SELF-HEALING
REIKI

SELF-HEALING
REIKI

Freeing the Symbols, Attunements, and Techniques

Your complete
home study course
for Reiki I, Reiki II,
and Reiki Master.

BARBARA EMERSON

FROG, LTD.
BERKELEY, CALIFORNIA

Self-Healing Reiki

Published by Frog, Ltd.
Frog, Ltd. books are distributed by
North Atlantic Books
P.O. Box 12327
Berkeley, CA 94712

Cover art © Ayelet Maida
Cover and book design © Ayelet Maida, A/M Studios
Reiki symbol drawings by Ed Betzel
Photographs of Reiki positions by Barbara Emerson
Printed in the United States of America

Self-Healing Reiki videos are available through North Atlantic Books by mail, phone, or info@northatlanticbooks.com

Reiki I	12:40 minutes	$25.00
Reiki II	14:40 minutes	$50.00
Reiki Master	16:00 minutes	$75.00

North Atlantic Books are available through most bookstores.
To contact North Atlantic directly, call 800-337-2665 or visit our website at www.northatlanticbooks.com.

Substantial discounts on bulk quantities of North Atlantic books are available to corporations, professional associations, and other organizations. For details and discount information, contact the special sales department at North Atlantic Books.

Library of Congress Cataloging-in-Publication Data
Emerson, Barbara, 1944–
    Self healing reiki: freeing the symbols, attunements, and techniques/
by Barbara Emerson.
        p. cm.
    ISBN 1-58394-035-9 (alk. paper)
    1. Reiki (Healing system) 2. Self-care, Health. I. Title: Reiki. II. Title.
RZ403.R45 E46 2000
615.8'52—dc21
                                                    00-062296

3 4 5 6 7 8 9 10 MALLOY 07 06 05 04 03

Contents

Introduction **VII**

ONE The Reiki Legend **3**

TWO Reiki and Change **10**

THREE All About Reiki **15**

FOUR Energy **28**

FIVE Reiki I **38**

SIX Reiki II **56**

SEVEN Reiki III: The Masters Course **92**

EIGHT Teaching Reiki **117**

EPILOGUE Namaste Beloved One **140**

About the Author **142**

Introduction

During the mid-1800s a Japanese teacher, Mikao Usui, was on a mission to discover the process that Jesus Christ and other great healers used to heal. While studying ancient Sanskrit writings, Dr. Usui discovered this healing modality and called it Reiki. In Japanese, Reiki means "universal life force."

The difference between Reiki (pronounced "ray-key") and other healing modalities is the attunement process, an integral part of Reiki. The attunement instantly creates a pathway for energy to flow from the crown, through the heart, and exit through the hands. Through this process the student is able to feel the energy flowing and exiting through his or her hands. Before this book and accompanying video were published, the only way to receive an attunement was personally from a Reiki master.

Although Reiki is becoming more popular worldwide, there are still many areas where no Reiki master is available. It became my personal quest to discover a way to make the attunement process available to everyone, everywhere. After years of study I discovered a method of performing quality long-distance attunements. From long-distance attunements, it was a logical step to try to videotape the attunement process. Again, after a period of trial and error, I perfected the video attunement process. Now, in addition to this workbook, video attunements are available through the publisher.

Self-Healing Reiki is designed as a home study course. Divided into easy-to-understand modules, the book allows you, the reader, to advance from a Reiki novice to a Reiki master at your own pace.

Self-Healing Reiki presents a detailed history of Reiki, thoroughly explains energy and its application to healing, and walks you through each level of Reiki practice. Many other books have attached an eastern philosophy or New Age dogma to Reiki, thereby diluting the concept. Reiki is the healing modality used by all great healers throughout the centuries. It needs nothing else added to it to make it work. Attaching other concepts or philosophies to it does Reiki an injustice and often confuses its true meaning.

Self-Healing Reiki is a book about Reiki and nothing else. This presentation is unique because it: negates the concept of duality present in traditional Reiki teachings; publishes the traditional and nontraditional attunement processes; allows anyone with the desire to become a practitioner the opportunity to do so; is affordable; validates the role of the practitioner; is easy to read and practical to use; teaches pure Reiki with no other dogma or belief system attached; fills a void in areas where there are no Reiki masters to teach and attune students.

Reiki is much more than a healing system. It is the basis of all spirituality. Just imagine the attunement process as a huge electrical plug. When you receive an attunement, you are plugged directly into Source. What else is needed? You now have direct access to the Source of all creation, all the power of the universe, all the knowledge of the universe, all there is. The master course of *Self-Healing Reiki* teaches you how to work in the spiritual plane in order to consciously, consistently create your life. You need no other course.

There is an old saying: "There is nothing new under the sun." The material I am presenting here is not new, although the way it is viewed and presented may be. Everyone has access to all the knowledge in the universe. *Self-Healing Reiki* teaches us to allow ourselves to accept this knowledge and then have the courage to act upon what we know. With an open mind and heart, I invite you to journey with me to a new and different Reiki healing system.

Namaste. (The God I am recognizes the God you are.)

CHAPTER ONE

The Reiki Legend

There is a destiny that
makes us brothers.
None goes his way alone.
All that we send into the lives of others
Comes back into
our own.

—Edward Markam, *The Treasure Chest*

The Reiki story begins in the mid 1800s with a teacher, Dr. Makao Usui, searching for the ancient healing system used by Christ, Buddha, and all the ancient great healers. Dr. Usui, a Japanese scholar and philosopher, was educated by missionaries, became a Christian, and eventually rose to a position of eminence as head of a Christian boys' school in Kyoto. While working in his dual role of minister and principal, Dr. Usui was politely questioned by several of his senior students. They asked if he believed the Bible, literally. When Dr. Usui replied he did, they wanted him to demonstrate his belief by performing a miracle, one such as Jesus performed. As Dr. Usui was unable to do this, his students declared his to be an empty faith and insufficient to bolster their own. They stated that they needed more than blind faith in order to believe.

Dr. Usui was struck with the enormity of his position and asked the young men not to lose their faith. He declared his intention to immediately resign his position and travel to a Christian country of the West, where he was sure he would learn how to perform the miracles of Jesus. He would then return to give literal proof of his beliefs.

Dr. Usui traveled to America and enrolled in a Christian university in Chicago to study, in depth, the Christian scriptures. His interest was in the healing miracles recorded in the scripture.

When it became apparent he could not learn from the scriptures how Jesus healed, he began to explore the sacred writings of the other great world religions.

Learning that Buddha and his early disciples had performed healings, Dr. Usui began concentrating on the Buddhist writings. After seven years in America, Dr. Usui decided to return to Kyoto to further his studies of the Buddhist sutras. He often roamed the countryside visiting temples and monasteries. The monks he talked to were in agreement that Buddha healed many. But, they informed him, this practice had been dropped from Buddhism. The monks now concerned themselves only with spiritual health, leaving physical healing to the doctors.

During his search Dr. Usui met a Zen abbot, who invited him to live in his monastery while pursuing his studies. Dr. Usui remained with these monks and, legend has it, became a Zen monk. After studying the sutras in Japanese, he learned Chinese to see if he could get a clearer translation, since Buddhism was brought to Japan from China. He knew he was closer but had not yet found his answer. Dr. Usui decided to learn Sanskrit to be able to read the sutras in their original language. He had found the symbols, yet he did not know how to activate them or what to do with them.

Dr. Usui decided to go a few miles outside Kyoto to a mountain considered sacred by the monks. There he fasted and meditated in expectation of being shown the meaning of the information he had found. He discussed this with the abbot and told him that if, after twenty-one days, he did not return, to send some monks to collect his bones. He did not intend to return without an answer.

On the first day he piled twenty-one stones at the entrance of his cave. Every day he removed one stone to mark the passage of the days. After twenty days of intense meditation, nothing happened. On the final morning of his quest, in the darkest hour just before dawn, Dr. Usui stood in his cave and saw a tremendous projectile of light coming straight toward him. His first response was fear and a desire to run from it, but he reconsidered and decided this might be the answer to his quest. He stood motionless, determined to allow this experience, even if it should mean his death. The light struck his third eye, and he lost consciousness for a period of time.

As he regained consciousness he saw "millions and millions of bubbles in all the colors of the rainbow" with the Reiki symbols superimposed on the bubbles. He not only saw the symbols, he was also given their meaning and the information on how to activate this healing modality. The first Reiki attunement in the modern age was given and received. It was the psychic rediscovery of an ancient healing method. Dr. Usui named this newly awakened healing system Reiki. Rei means "universal" and Ki means "life force" in Japanese. The healing system remains universal.

As Dr. Usui rushed to return to Kyoto, he stubbed his toe quite painfully. Eager to put what he had learned to the test he grabbed his toe, used his newfound healing energy, and experienced an instant healing. This was his first validation of the truth of his vision.

As he continued down the mountain, he realized he was hungry. He stopped at a roadside food stand and was served a meal by the owner's granddaughter. Her face was swollen, and she was in much pain from an infected tooth. Dr. Usui asked permission to touch her cheek, and as he did, the girl's pain immediately ceased, and the swelling went down. This healing proved that Reiki worked on others as easily as it had worked on him.

When Dr. Usui returned to the monastery, he learned that the abbot was in great pain from arthritis. As soon as Dr. Usui had bathed and dressed in clean robes, he visited the abbot and relieved the abbot's pain. Dr. Usui was now sure the ancient healing arts used by all great masters had been unearthed.

Dr. Usui practiced and taught Reiki in Japan for the rest of his life. There is now some speculation that Dr. Usui first taught Reiki without using attunements. In the beginning he taught Reiki as a long process in which the students learned Reiki as they lived with and studied with the master. Students lived with Dr. Usui until he felt they had learned and practiced all there was to know about Reiki. After this learning period he elevated them to masters and sent them out into the community to perform healings.

Dr. Usui was a member of a spiritual group called Rei Jyutsu Ka and his adepts lived and worked daily with him, as the apostles did with Christ.

It is thought that the attunement process was started when Dr. Usui began training lay people, beginning with a naval officer by the name of Chujiro Hayashi. Dr. Usui apparently felt that since lay people did not have the benefit of living and working alongside the masters, they required a process to attune them to the energy. Dr. Usui had received his attunement on Mt. Kyoto. It is said Dr. Usui attuned seventeen Reiki masters using the attunement process. No one knows how many masters he initiated in his monastery.

Before his death Dr. Usui formulated his Five Spiritual Precepts. These are the precepts all Reiki practitioners live by:

1. Just for today, I will not anger.
2. Just for today, I will not worry.
3. Just for today, I will give thanks for my many blessings.
4. Just for today, I will do my work honestly.
5. Just for today, I will be kind to all living things.

According to legend, Chujiro Hayashi was the first lay person to receive an attunement and was Dr. Usui's most dedicated student. He became the next Reiki grand master, carrying on the tradition of teaching and healing. Hayashi operated several Reiki healing centers in Japan. One of his clients was a Hawaiian woman of Japanese descent named Hawaka Takata. This very ill woman was destined to play an amazing part in the emergence of Reiki as a worldwide healing modality.

Mrs. Takata was born on a plantation in Kauai, Hawaii. Her parents were Japanese immigrants and worked in the sugarcane fields. She lost her husband in 1930 and worked very hard to provide financial security for her family. Finally she suffered a nervous breakdown from overwork. Added to this, she had a painful abdominal condition that required surgery, complicated by a respiratory problem, which prevented the use of anesthetics. Her doctor told her that she must have the surgery or she would die, and since he believed she would not survive the operation, he refused to take responsibility for it.

Before Mrs. Takata could decide about the pending surgery, her sister died. She was forced to accompany her sister's body to Japan for burial in their ancestral burial ground. After services for her sister, Mrs. Takata went to Tokyo and entered a small private hospital in Akasaka. After a thorough examination it was determined that Mrs. Takata was suffering from a stomach tumor, gallstones, and appendicitis. She was scheduled for surgery at seven o'clock the next morning.

As Mrs. Takata was lying on the surgical table waiting for surgery, she quite clearly heard a voice say, "The operation is not necessary. The operation is not necessary." She slipped off the table and, with a sheet wrapped around her, asked the head surgeon if he knew of any other treatment to help her. He sent for his sister, who was also the hospital dietitian. She took Mrs. Takata by streetcar to another section of the city and introduced her to the wife of Reiki grand master Chujiro Hayashi.

Mrs. Takata started Reiki treatments, with one man working on her abdomen and another working on her head. She could hear them commenting on what they were sensing. While they were making their observations, she could feel the heat from their hands.

The next day before Mrs. Takata lay down on the couch for her treatment, she looked under it to see if there were wires connected to some sort of instrument or battery creating heat. Then she looked at the ceiling to see if there were wires above. There were none, so she assumed the practitioners must have had instruments in their pockets to cause the heat she was feeling.

As treatment began, Mrs. Takata reached up and grabbed the pocket of one of her practitioners. Startled, he asked her what she was doing. She replied that she was looking for the instrument supplying the heat in the treatment. The practitioner explained to her that no instruments were used, only their hands. He explained that Reiki practitioners are in tune with the universal life force. It is this force coming through their hands and entering the recipient's body that creates the heat.

After several months of treatments, Mrs. Takata was completely healed. At this point Mrs. Takata had an intense desire to become a Reiki practitioner, but being a woman and a foreigner, she knew this was impossible. Then, as often happens in our lives, the decision was taken out of her hands.

Dr. Hayashi was a retired naval officer, and he kept in contact with world situations. Fearing a war would engulf his beloved Japan, he made a decision to attune Mrs. Takata and allow her to become the first female Reiki practitioner in the world. In this way he knew that if Japan were destroyed, Reiki would live on.

She was the last master Dr. Hayashi attuned, and she eventually became the next Reiki grand master upon his death. Mrs. Takata returned to Hawaii in 1937 and established Reiki in this hemisphere. Prior to her death in 1980, she initiated twenty-two Reiki masters. This was the beginning of Reiki as we know it. We all owe Mrs. Takata a debt of gratitude.

REVIEW

- Reiki is a holistic healing modality rediscovered in the mid 1800s by Dr. Usui. It is the exact same healing modality used by all the great, ancient healers including Buddha and Jesus Christ.

- Reiki was originally practiced in Japan and women were not allowed to be practitioners. All of this changed after Mrs. Takata was healed with Reiki. Mrs. Takata was a Hawaiian-born woman of Japanese descent. She suffered from a multitude of physical problems and traveled to Japan for surgery. Instead she was introduced to Reiki and after several months was healed.

- Dr. Hayashi, a retired naval officer and Reiki grand master, saw the war clouds on the horizon and was afraid Reiki would be lost if his beloved Japan entered the war. To safeguard the Reiki teachings, he taught and attuned Mrs. Takata to the Reiki master level.

- Mrs. Takata returned to Hawaii and brought Reiki to this hemisphere. For forty-three years she established Reiki clinics, healed thousands of people, and became the first female Reiki master. Before her death, she personally attuned twenty-two Reiki masters.

- Mrs. Takata lived, healed, and taught Reiki; she shielded and nourished the Reiki embryo she brought with her from Japan into the wonderful universal holistic system in use today.

CHAPTER TWO

Reiki and Change

As Adam early in the morning
Walking forth from the bower
refresh'd with sleep,
Behold me where I pass,
hear my voice, approach,
Touch me, touch the palm of your hand
to my body as I pass,
Be not afraid of my body.

—Walt Whitman, *Leaves of Grass*

It is thought that Mrs. Takata taught Reiki as a closely guarded subject, surrounding the Reiki symbols and attunements with secrecy. The students were not allowed to keep their notes; all were destroyed at the end of the class. Therefore the students had to rely on their memory to recall the information taught. For many years Reiki was taught exactly as it was taught by Mrs. Takata with no leeway given for new thoughts or ideas. This rigidity caused traditional Reiki to become obsolete and nontraditional Reiki practices to become popular.

It is human nature to process knowledge in our own particular way. It is also human nature to forget some of the things we are taught, especially complicated symbols and attunement processes. I believe that a lot of information was forgotten or, because the teacher was not sure, just eliminated. I know of Reiki masters who have expelled students from their classes for questioning or wanting to change or modify a hand position.

Now Reiki is evolving. Old concepts are being remembered, new concepts are being added, so Reiki is a "work in progress." This new attitude allows the masters leeway in their presentations. Teaching Reiki in the traditional manner limits the power of Reiki. Traditional Reiki masters teach that there is only one right way to practice Reiki. By doing so, they are trying to limit the limitless. Source manifests itself in many, many ways. Since Source is manifesting through each Reiki practitioner, its powers can by taught in various ways.

Traditional Reiki teaches that the purpose of an attunement is to open and align the student to the Source energy and allow Source energy to enter and flow through the student's body, thereby making the student a channel or vessel. By teaching that the practitioner is just a conduit for the energy and does not assist in the healing in any way, traditional Reiki is teaching duality. Source is not separate from or outside of ourselves. To believe it is invalidates humankind, separates us, in thought from who we really are—Source.

This realization came to me several years ago when I was teaching a Reiki Master class. We were discussing attunements, and I said, "An attunement opens the student's crown to receive the healing energy of Source. Once the crown is opened, the Source energy flows through the practitioner, and goes where it is needed. The practitioner is only a conduit for this healing energy." I stopped in my tracks as the implication of what I had just said hit me. I was teaching duality! I had been trained to teach that Source is outside of us, that attunements open us to that external Source, that we, as practitioners, are nothing but a vessel to allow this external Source to do its work. But it's not true. Source dwells within us. We are the vehicles Source uses to incarnate as human beings.

The attunement process allows us to make contact with, recognize, and feel the God within while releasing the blocks and fears preventing us from realizing who and what we are. Then the God within combines with the God without to flow through our bodies to heal the client, or flow through the universe to heal anyone, anytime, anywhere. Source is indivisible. I had separated the Source within and the Source without to explain the union of all of Source that occurs when we are attuned. But we are not only vessels for the healing power; we are active participants in the healing process—always, always, always.

As a Reiki practitioner you are intimately involved in the healing process. You are the person who actively guides those in need of healing to the Reiki energy. You open yourself and allow the Source energy to enter your body, mix with the Source energy within you, and exit out of your hands. You are the one who is working on this earth plane to bring the knowledge of the Reiki healing energy to the world. Without you and every other practitioner in the world, there would be no Reiki healings.

When we are attuned, we are opened to the ultimate creative power of the universe, and as such we are limitless in what we can accomplish. Nothing we do can alter this power in any way. We are in a partnership, working in conjunction with universal Source to heal the world, one person at a time.

The Reiki practitioner stands between the worlds. One hand is raised drawing all the energy from the universe and pulling it into his or her body. This universal energy then mixes with the energy within the practitioner and exits out of the right hand, which is pointed at the earth. The Reiki practitioner is the link allowing universal Source to personally enter our universe and heal our world.

Some Reiki masters feel threatened by the evolution of Reiki. There are so many new concepts, symbols, and ways of doing attunements that it seems the very foundation of Reiki is threatened. Actually what is happening is the light of Source is illuminating the closed system. Yes, changes are occurring in attitudes, in the way Reiki is being taught; yes, in the way attunements are given, and in the cost of learning Reiki. Does Reiki need to evolve to grow? Yes.

Reiki is for everyone. My burning desire is to make Reiki available to anyone who has the desire to practice it. There is room and need for everyone's interpretation of Reiki. I honor everyone who is trying to make a difference in this world by teaching Reiki to the best of his or her ability and according to his or her conscience. There is a lot of work to be done, and it can only be done if we honor and respect everyone who is trying to accomplish the task.

Since the healing art of Reiki was rediscovered by Dr. Usui, it has been a closed fraternity with certain, strict rules of conduct. Chief among these was that Reiki knowledge, symbols, and attunements were to be kept secret, revealed only to those who could afford the oftentimes prohibitive price of the Reiki courses.

Diane Stein is credited with ripping the veil of secrecy off Reiki by publishing the Reiki symbols. By doing so she began the process of making Reiki available to all who have a desire to heal themselves and others. I heartily salute her for her courage and honor her knowledge. Although her book made the body of knowledge available to everyone, there was still the problem of getting an attunement without access to a Reiki master.

I took this problem to my Reiki guides and was shown how to perform *long-distance and video attunements*. It made complete sense. If we could (and we do) use Reiki power to send healings long-distance, why couldn't we send attunements long-distance? Why couldn't a Reiki master charge a videotape with the attunement energy to allow anyone who views it to receive an attunement? With this knowledge, the last roadblock to making Reiki available to everyone was removed and an important aspect of my home-study course was born.

I first perfected long-distance attunements. I have students all over the world whom I attuned from my home in Arizona. Although these attunements have been vastly successful, it still did not solve the problem of people with no access to a master. In order to receive a long-distance attunement from me, the student and I had to be in contact with each other. So I decided that if long-distance healing works, and long-distance attunements work, then putting the attunement on video and energizing the video has to work. I sent out my videos and had students try this new attunement process. I was shocked at how effortlessly and successfully these videotapes worked. The videotapes may be used in conjunction with this workbook.

There are universal laws of energy. One basic law is that if one type of energy can be transmitted in a certain way, then all types of energy can be transmitted the same way. I believe we are Source and in contact with Source while practicing Reiki, so how could we possibly limit what Source is capable of?

REVIEW

When Mrs. Takata brought Reiki to this hemisphere and first started teaching Reiki, she taught it as a closed, secret system. No student could take his or her notes out of the classroom. The students had to rely on the memory of the material originally taught. The original Reiki masters propagated this method of teaching. There was no leeway given for new thoughts or ideas. Reiki soon became a stagnant healing modality. Today, people who can trace their lineage back to Mrs. Takata are called traditional Reiki masters or practitioners.

As the world evolved, so did Reiki. There are now thousands of non-traditional Reiki masters and practitioners who are embracing new thoughts and ideas.

New ideas are being revealed almost daily. The Internet, with its instant communication ability, has united Reiki practitioners all over the world to share their ideas and ways of practicing Reiki. Information that was lost is now being retrieved and circulated around the world.

Through new attunement methods Reiki has now become available to everyone, anywhere in the world. You no longer have to be physically present with a Reiki master to receive your attunement. This fact alone has advanced the availability of Reiki tremendously. Now, for the first time, anyone who can read a book or view a video can become a Reiki practitioner.

CHAPTER THREE

All About Reiki

In the beginning there was desire,
which was the first seed of mind;
sages, having meditated in their hearts
have discovered by their wisdom,
the connection of the existent
with the non existent.

—The Hymn of Creation, *The Rig Veda*

Reiki means "universal life force." There is an energy field surrounding everything in our universe. Reiki is a healing technique that utilizes this universal life force energy to heal the body at all levels: physical, mental, emotional, and spiritual. There are just as many names for this life force as there are civilizations.

The person who is attuned as a Reiki practitioner has his or her body's energy channels opened and cleared of obstructions by the Reiki attunements. Now the student not only awakens the life energy within but also receives an increase in this life energy, or Ki, for his or her own healing while becoming connected to the source of all universal Ki. It is always a combination of Source within and universal Source doing the healing.

What Reiki Is

Reiki is Source, the universal life force energy. It is this energy that created the universe and all within it. Pretty powerful stuff! Reiki is one of the few forms of healing that can be used to heal yourself. Reiki never conflicts with traditional medical treatments, but facilitates and enhances them. Reiki speeds the recovery process and is a source of energy during illness.

Reiki is free and available at all times. This means if you get sick at three in the morning, help is always available. Reiki is energy in pure form, is always present at the same power level, and will work on or with anything it is directed to—plants, animals, cars, flashlights, or anything else.

When I was a brand-new Reiki level II practitioner, I went on a woman's retreat sponsored by my Reiki master. We would all get up very early in the morning to meditate together. My master would read different verses each morning to prepare us for the days' activities. On the second morning, just as she was preparing to read the day's verse, the flashlight went out as I was holding it. My master looked at me and nodded her head. I looked at her and shook my head no. She looked back at me, a little sterner, and emphatically nodded her head. I shrugged my shoulders, turned my Reiki healing energy on, and the flashlight turned on brighter than before. I held the flashlight on her page all during the reading. When she was finished, I put the flashlight down, and it immediately shut off. Does Reiki work on batteries? Yes!

Reiki energy is always ready for use, anytime, or anywhere. Reiki is a technique for directing, balancing, and restoring natural life force energy for yourself and others. No special environment is needed, no special equipment is needed, and anyone can be taught to become a Reiki practitioner. Reiki cannot violate anyone's free will. If the energy is refused, then Reiki cannot enter their energy field. It is a matter of choice, and the choice is always the client's.

Reiki is the greatest teacher for those willing to listen and learn. Much more will be gained through your actual experience of Reiki as you move through life than could ever be written or described. As you begin to live in the natural energy flow of this healing, illuminating, balancing, and invigorating energy, this teaching will take on deeper and deeper meaning. Reread this book as many times as you wish. Long ago I started the practice of highlighting passages in books that resonate to me using a different color for each reading. After several readings, some of my books have almost every passage highlighted in a rainbow of colors. Each time we reread a book we are at a different place, so different passages resonate to us. Sometimes we need to listen to all of the passages.

Reiki enhances everything it touches. It cannot interfere with medications or regimens a person is taking from allopathic medicine. There is a surgeon in my hometown of Mesa, Arizona, who gives his patients a Reiki healing treatment before, during, and after surgery. Do his patients do better than those of other surgeons? You bet.

The person receiving the healing does not have to believe in Reiki. If that person gives permission for the healing and is open to it, the healing happens. But someone who is not open to receiving the energy can consciously or unconsciously block the process. If the person refuses the energy, the healer can do no more.

A very dear friend of mine was diagnosed with cancer of the bone. I went to her house and performed a Reiki treatment. It went well and we agreed I would continue the treatments until she was cured. When I knocked on her door the next day, she could not look me in the eye. She said we would have to discontinue treatments. When I asked her why, she said that when she was receiving the treatment the day before she had seen hundreds of purple bubbles in her mind. She was afraid I was spreading her cancer! I tried to explain that the purple bubbles represented healing and the treatment was working, but her mind was made up and she refused to change it. Did I stop the treatments? Yes. Does she still have cancer? Yes. Can I help her? No, not without her permission. Am I sad? Yes.

Reiki will not interfere with medications or other procedures, other than to make them more effective and the patient more comfortable. Reiki enhances whatever it touches.

Reiki is a powerful, natural system that unlocks the inner flow of vital energy within the practitioner and allows him or her to direct this flow where needed. It is an effective way of creating and maintaining wellness, thus reducing or eliminating the cost of health care and controlling the anxiety often associated with a disease process or the act of dying.

Reiki is a technique for balancing natural energy. If we are out of balance, we are in a dis-ease state, meaning "out of ease." Reiki energy restores balance and aligns our energy centers to create a state of "ease" or health. In this way, using Reiki on ourselves daily keeps us in a state of balance and therefore a state of health. Reiki is also a preventive and maintenance tool for our healthy state of being.

Reiki is a powerful, dynamic tool for personal growth and spiritual enlightenment. Since the attunements open your consciousness to the Source within and puts you in direct contact with universal Source, using Reiki as an adjunct to any other personal growth tools or spiritual tools you are using will enhance whatever you are trying to accomplish.

What Reiki is not

Reiki is not difficult to use, since intuitively we always place our hands on any part of our body that hurts, if we can. The only difference is that after an attunement, Source is combining with our inner energy and sending healing energy through our hands.

Reiki is not psychic healing, mind control, or hypnosis. It is not a form of mental healing; therefore, belief structures do not enter in to the picture. Reiki never attempts to control your mind or belief systems, nor does it try to affect your thinking processes.

Reiki is not a dogma or belief. Although a lot of masters tie their particular belief system to Reiki, there are no religious connotations, thoughts, or dogmas attached to Reiki energy.

Neither is Reiki laying on of hands or hands-on healing. The Reiki flow is started with the practitioner's intent to use the Reiki energy. There is no need to lay on hands to start the flow. Reiki can be used for healings across time and in other dimensions. It is a form of pure energy. Can you imagine how long your arms would have to be to reach across the world?

Reiki is not imagery, visualization, or wishful thinking. It is not only for when you are sick. Daily use of Reiki will fine-tune your body and energy field to act as a barrier to any disease process lurking around. It is a daily shot of energy! It is not a massage technique, although many massage therapists combine Reiki with their massage techniques for optimum results. Reiki enhances all it touches, including massage.

Reiki never drains or depletes the practitioner's energy. You, as a practitioner, are attuned to a limitless supply of energy. What sets Reiki apart from any other healing system is the attunement process. Therefore, to be properly trained, you must be attuned.

Video attunements use the same principles that make long-distance healing possible. *If one is possible, then the other has to be.* I have been performing long-distance and video attunements successfully for over a year and these attunements are just as strong as any I have performed when the student has been physically present. As a matter of fact, I feel I am more focused when performing long-distance or video attunements than I am when I attune a student who is sitting in front of me. It is not my position to limit Source by saying that something is impossible when dealing with the most powerful energy in the universe. If Reiki is for everyone, then there must be a way to attune everyone, even those not physically close to a Reiki master. Video attunements use the same techniques as any other attunement. The master charges the video and the attunement is passed when the student views the video.

How does Reiki work?

Everything on this planet is a form of energy, even rocks! A Reiki attunement connects the receiver to the limitless supply of energy called Source by establishing a physical pathway for the energy to enter and flow within the body. Upon receiving your first attunement in Reiki level I, you become awakened to the energy within and therefore become a carrier for this limitless, universal energy. From the time of your first attunement, and for the rest of your life, all you need to do to connect to this energy is to have the intent to use Reiki. Your thoughts and intentions are the on-and-off switch for Reiki.

One of my students, a Reiki master, likes to tell this story. Her son and grandchildren were in a very bad automobile accident. Upon release from the hospital, the three-year-old kept asking his grandmother to fix his boo-boos. She finally asked him if he would like to learn how to make himself feel better. He readily answered yes! She gave him the attunement and showed him how to put his hands on himself, but he became puzzled when she tried to explain intent to him. Finally, she just told him that when he wanted to use Reiki, he should just say, "Reiki on." That's exactly what we do when we have the intent to use Reiki.

The attunement, by combining the Source within with the universal life Source, also increases your life force energy. You will experience an energy that first heals you and then heals others, without depleting anyone's energy level. Using Reiki should never deplete your own energy level. If it does, contact your Reiki master and have your energy channels checked. The attunement process immediately establishes a pathway for the energy to travel from the crown to the heart, where it divides and exits out of the hands. While other healing modalities can form this pathway, it often takes years to form.

There are many healing modalities in use today. Each of them works because we all tap into the same Source of power. The huge difference is, with Reiki, the energy is always consistent. I had a very dear friend who was a healer long before I ever found Reiki. Once I became a practitioner, I would tell her she must try Reiki. She would always reply, "I was healing people while you were still in diapers." I acknowledged that this was true but insisted she still should try Reiki. About six months later I received a call from her. She said she became a Reiki practitioner, and there was a tremendous difference in her healing sessions. She said that without the Reiki attunements, her healing energy felt sporadic, sometimes strong and sometimes weak. After she received her attunements, the energy consistently left her hands at the same strength, no matter how many treatments she did a day.

The attunement process is a shortcut to what used to take years, maybe lifetimes, to accomplish. With an attunement you actually physically experience and attract the energy of creation. The radical change in your own vibrational field allows you to harmonize with Source energy.

The attunement does not give the healer anything new: it opens and aligns what is already a part of you. The process is much like plugging in a lamp in a house already wired for electricity. When you are attuned, you have plugged your energy system into the universal Source and can cause this energy to flow, just like turning on the light switch in a house. Your body was already wired for Reiki; all you had to do was plug it in. The attunement is your plug. Reiki is part of your genetic code, and when you study Reiki you are actually remembering what is an intuitive part of yourself.

A common comparison is Reiki and television. When I turn on my television set, I do not know how all those little dots travel through space, somehow bounce off satellites, find my television screen, and appear in the proper order to form pictures. They not only form pictures; they are in color and moving. It is the same with Reiki. I do not know exactly how the energy works, I only know that it does.

In direct-contact healing, the energy is transmitted through the hands of one who has been attuned to practice Reiki. This person is now referred to as a practitioner. The practitioner allows all of Source energy to enter his or her body, combine with his or her own Source energy, and pass through his or her body via the hands, to the body of the client. By so doing, the practitioner is an active participant in the healing process.

There is no ego involved in performing this function. Is this person a healer? Definitely. According to Taber's medical dictionary, a healer is one who heals by use of an alternative method such as spiritual healing, or through holistic medicine.

Let's define holistic medicine: It is the comprehensive and total care of the patient. In this system, the needs of the patient in all areas—physical, emotional, spiritual, social, and economic—are considered and cared for. This definition comes from a medical dictionary! So, as a Reiki practitioner, are you a healer? You bet.

How is Reiki taught?

Reiki is divided into three levels. Reiki I is a self-healing modality. In Reiki I you are taught the legend of Reiki, hand positions, and how Reiki works. You also receive your first attunement. This attunement forms a pathway, which allows Source energy to enter into your body and combine with your own Source energy and exit out of your body. The opening of the crown symbolically gives permission to universal life force energy to enter your body. Remember that nothing can happen to us without our permission. The attunement immediately creates a pathway from your crown to your heart for the flow of this energy. Your heart is then opened to allow a combining of the universal life force energy and your own internal Source energy. This energy is then released from the body via the hands. For the first time you can actually feel the energy and know it is something always within you. In Reiki I the attunement itself heals physical level diseases in the person who receives it and allows the emotional source of their dis-ease to surface and be dealt with. Reiki I healing sessions are primarily for self-healing. The Reiki I practitioner can also do healing sessions for someone who is physically present.

Reiki II takes you one step further and teaches you how to use Reiki to heal others and how to send energy to the future or use the energy to change the past. Since humans create the illusion of time, Reiki II teaches you to advance through time or travel back in time, at your discretion.

Reiki is now not only transmitted through your hands but through your thought processes as well. With your thoughts you now can send energy anywhere, in any fashion you choose. You can even access your timeline simply by thinking about it! You will learn three Reiki symbols, what they mean, and how and when to use them. You will receive another attunement that vastly increases the power of the Reiki energy. The Reiki II attunement completes the forming of the pathway of universal life force energy from the head to the heart and out through the hands. The Reiki II symbols are transferred to your hands and Reiki is now sealed in you for life. At this stage you can start charging for your healing sessions and, if you choose, make your living as a Reiki practitioner or supplement your income by offering Reiki.

The Reiki II attunement increases the power of the healing energy flowing through your body. Basically, Reiki I connects you with the energy within you and establishes the flow of energy from the crown to the heart and, to a limited degree, out of your hands. Reiki II completes the flow by opening the hands to allow the energy to enter your crown, combine with your internal energy, and flow freely out your hands. Crown, heart, and hand connections are now complete.

After this attunement old emotions, unhealed former situations, and negative mental patterns may resurface to be healed at last. This surfacing of buried emotions can take as long as six months to the rest of your life to complete. Though not always comfortable, the process is positive and necessary. Healing with Reiki II adds considerable power to direct sessions, because the complete circuit is open. The Reiki II attunement also allows us to control the flow and destination of the energy by our intent. You no longer have to be physically present to perform a healing.

Reiki III is the masters and trainers degree. A master is simply a teacher, one who has mastered a discipline. No ego or ownership is otherwise involved in the term. The Reiki III attunement involves spiritual-level energy and activates a spiritual healing in the person receiving it. This energy is pure joy, oneness with all life, and a firm connection to Source. Reiki III includes two more symbols and teaches the methods of passing on the attunements. This degree is only recommended for the serious healer, and especially for those who want to make Reiki a major part of their lives. When you become a Reiki master, you accept the responsibility of training others to become practitioners and masters.

After you are attuned to each degree of Reiki, you will undergo a period of healing in your own life. I refer to this as the cleansing or detox period. Each attunement changes the vibrational levels of your human body, and the body often reacts to it. You also may feel changes on the mental or emotional level. As the Source energy is awakened and recognized within you and moves and works through you, it automatically cleanses you. Think of a chimney sweep. The powerful sweep cleans the sticky, hard creosote formed in the chimney, so the more subtle smoke can rise through it. It is the same with us. When we are attuned, Reiki, the powerful chimney sweep, cleanses and aligns our being so the more subtle healing energy is not impeded when it is flowing through us to the recipient. Remember, Reiki is a healing art for the practitioner also. Every time you practice Reiki you are healing, balancing, and loving yourself.

During the period of detoxification after each attunement you may feel spacey or tingly, have intense dreams, or experience upset stomach symptoms. Your body is adjusting to the vibrational energy changes caused by the attunement. There is an increase in your capacity to allow the energy to flow from and through you. More energy is entering your aura and body than you have ever experienced before, and your body is reacting to this change in its vibrational level.

When Reiki doesn't appear to work

There will be times when it appears that Reiki is not working. Neither you nor the client can feel any flow and there doesn't seem to be any exchange of energy. There could be several reasons for this apparent lack of action:

1. Although the client stated that she or he wanted the Reiki session, she or he could be unconsciously blocking the energy, through fear or ignorance of the procedure. Simply explain the process and try again.

2. Sometimes death is the cure. We do not live forever. If our client's body is ready to make the transition from life to death, a Reiki healing session can ease this process. Oftentimes when this is occurring, there is no healing energy felt by the client. Even so, be assured the energy is assisting the client in the emotional and mental areas and preparing him or her for death. Reiki often removes the fear of death in people, so they become more peaceful and accepting of their transition.

3. The client does not want to give up the disease process, so as quickly as she or he is healed; she or he manifests the disease again. This means she or he is just not ready to be healed.

4. There are times when no apparent result occurs immediately, but the next day the client notices a difference in the way she or he feels. This means it took a little time for the results of the session to be felt.

5. Sometimes the healing takes place and the client isn't even aware of it. As a new Reiki master, I was offering free healing sessions at a Reiki practitioner's night. I was sitting on the floor when a young man came up to me and said, "I don't believe in this stuff, but I'm going to let you work on me anyway." I thought, "Gee thanks." As I was working on him, his body literally twitched and lifted off the floor several times. He thrashed around so much that the other practitioners were looking at us. When it was over and I asked him to sit up he said, "See, I didn't feel anything. I told you it wouldn't work!"

As a Reiki master and trainer, I live Reiki every day of my life. This doesn't mean I don't live my life, only that I am aware of my thoughts and actions. I am consciously aware of the things I do, the people I meet, and all of my surroundings. Living Reiki certainly does not make me a saint, guru, hermit, or any other label; it just makes me realize I am Source having a human experience. I know we are here to live each minute to the fullest and experience many different things. What Reiki enables me to do is to live non-judgmentally and realize that everyone is where he or she is supposed to be. Reiki enhances everything I do, and for that I am thankful. I firmly believe we are instinctively drawn to our Reiki masters. I thank you for your interest in Reiki and for choosing me as your master.

REVIEW

- Reiki is usually taught in three parts: Reiki I, Reiki II, and Reiki Master. In the most simplistic form, Reiki I is self-healing, Reiki II is healing others and long-distance healing, and Reiki Master is living Reiki daily and teaching others how to do the same.

- Reiki is a holistic healing modality which uses universal life force energy to restore balance to persons, places, or things. Since dis-ease means out of ease or balance, restoring balance puts the body back into a state of ease or health.

- Universal life force energy, which I refer to as Source, is pure energy. Everything in this universe is composed of energy. Therefore, Reiki not only restores health in animate objects, but also works equally well on inanimate objects. This means that you can use Reiki on everything.

- Reiki is the only holistic healing modality with an attunement process. The attunement creates a pathway for the external Source energy to enter through your crown, travel down to your heart where it mixes with your internal Source energy, and exit through your palms. This pathway can be created by repeated use of other healing practices, but it usually takes years to complete. The attunement process makes you and Source co-creators of healing energy.

- Reiki energy is never harmful. If you are taking any medicine or diet or therapy, Reiki only enhances whatever you are doing. On the other hand, never discontinue any medicine you may be taking because you feel so good with the Reiki healing energy. Never play doctor and always consult your doctor before you change anything you are doing.

- Reiki energy works, but not always in the way we expect. There may be times when the Reiki energy is not felt during a healing session. Know that this energy is working to facilitate healing, but it is just not visible yet. Healing dis-ease is comparable to peeling an onion, often there are layers of emotions attached to our dis-ease process. Be patient. You did not get sick in a day, and all too often you will not be healed in a day.

- Reiki is for everyone. You need no special skills or intelligence to learn Reiki. We are all healers; we need only to remember how to heal ourselves.

- Each one of us has free will and can decide what will be done to our bodies. The only time Reiki cannot work is when permission to enter your body is denied.

- Reiki is a completely natural healing system that is available anytime or anywhere. It requires no special equipment and always enhances whatever it touches.

CHAPTER FOUR

Energy

Each particle of matter
is an immensity;
each leaf a world,
each insect an
inexplicable compendium.

—Lavater, *The Treasure Chest*

Every person, place, or thing on this earth, in this galaxy and all the galaxies of the universe, is composed of energy. The rock, the chair, the fish, the man, the woman, the stars, everything, absolutely everything, is composed of energy.

According to Webster's dictionary, energy is manifested in various forms: motion (kinetic), position (potential energy), mass energy (atoms), pure energy (thought/spirit), light, heat, ionizing radiation, and sound. The theory that energy cannot be created or destroyed, but is often transformed into other forms, is called conservation. Kinetic energy is energy in motion; latent energy is energy that exists but is not being used. Potential energy is stored energy. Radiant energy is a form that is transmitted through space without the support of a sensible or defined medium.

The human body is composed of pure energy (usually referred to as spirit) and mass energy (atoms). The atom is the smallest building block of energy that can be accurately measured. Webster's dictionary states an atom is the smallest part of an element, consisting of a nucleus (protons and neurons), surrounded by electrons. The nucleus is positively charged, while the electrons are negatively charged. An atom is always in perfect balance. If you look at a drawing of an atom in a book or through a powerful microscope, it looks like a small world, which is exactly what it is! In other words, this basic building block of all creation allows the body or anything else to be seen, felt, and heard. The pure energy of Source, which is manifested as thought, is the creative force of the universe, and Source uses atoms to create what we desire.

Source is comprised of pure energy. This energy can be detected and measured but not seen by the naked eye. The Kirlian camera measures residual energy left by living entities. If I put a whole leaf on paper, then cut the leaf in half, and photograph the remaining half, the image of a whole leaf will appear. This demonstrates that the leaf is composed of energy, and even when a portion of the leaf is gone, its energy remains for a short period of time. If the experiment is repeated after a lapse of time, the energy will have dissipated, and only half a leaf will be shown. The Kirlian camera, invented in Russia, is a very efficient way to record and verify energy.

The aura camera photographs the body's energy. This energy is actually light-intensive vibrations emanating from the body. Within these vibrations we store all of our emotions, memories, thoughts, and behavioral patterns. These vibrations are in a constant state of motion and are always changing.

The aura photographer has you place your hands on a metal plate, which transfers the imprint of your energy to the film in a split second. The photograph is an image of your vibrational energy force recorded for one second. If you wear bright colors, these will be reflected in your photograph. If you are happy, scared, angry, or depressed, these emotions will be reflected through the camera. The aura changes as your thoughts, feelings, or emotions change.

Having an aura photograph taken can be fun and enlightening, depending on the quality of the camera and the expertise of the person reading the photo. A friend of mine takes and interprets aura photographs. One day I asked her what she tells the customer when she sees death or illness in a picture. She answered that people do not want to hear about death or illness, they just want to hear about how great they are, and that's exactly what she tells them. What you hear from the photographer may just be what they think you want to hear!

If energy has to be in perfect balance to function properly, what happens when that energy is somehow out of balance? When energy is in a state of balance, it is in a state of ease. When it is out of balance, it enters a state of dis-ease. Taber's medical dictionary literally defines disease as the lack of ease. Sound familiar?

There are many belief systems about how an illness occurs in the body. Some beliefs include "catching" the disease, deserving the punishment of a disease, the worn-out body causing illness, or creating our own illness. In order to explain how Reiki heals, I must explain the belief system that forms the basis of Reiki. Reiki works on the theory that everyone and everything is composed of energy, and that energy must be in balance to maintain health. Reiki eliminates dis-ease by correcting the energy imbalance, thereby reinstating the body to a state of ease. A thought is pure energy. When we attach a feeling to thought, we create an emotion. Being human, our emotions rule our bodies. That which we fear, we must always create!

Let me give you an example of the creation of fear. You walk into your house, turn on the television set, and see a serious-looking person standing in front of a map of the state or nation. The subject being discussed is about the latest outbreak of Foolyou flu. You are being told about the number of people who have already succumbed to the flu in the area where you live. You hear the symptoms—headache, sore throat, stomach upset, pain. As you hear these symptoms described, you start to feel a headache begin. Your throat becomes scratchy, and you think you too have probably caught the Foolyou flu. Then, miracles of miracles, the man is telling what you can take to help you get rid of this terrible flu, so you can sleep better tonight! You rush down to the drugstore and buy the product. By doing so, you have probably missed the announcement that this public service broadcast was sponsored by the same people who happen to make this wonderful remedy. Did they fool you?

What is an epidemic? An epidemic is the appearance of an infectious disease attacking many people at the same time in the same geographical area. According to Taber's Medical Dictionary, infectious means capable of being transmitted with or without contact, pertaining to a disease caused by a microorganism and producing infection.

If there is an epidemic or flu going around, you probably have been consciously or unconsciously bombarded with the knowledge that a lot of people are getting sick, maybe even dying. This thought has been planted in your unconscious mind. You may see the statistics in the paper, hear it on your radio or TV, or hear other people talking about it. You may even know someone who got the flu. The field is plowed, so to speak, and ready for the seed of illness to be planted in your unconscious mind. Your fertile imagination does the rest. As you think of getting sick, your wonderful body does whatever you ask it to and starts producing the symptoms. Your unconscious mind gives directions to your body to produce the symptoms of the illness, even though your conscious mind is not aware of these directions.

Now, let's look at how the belief system works to produce your symptoms. First, Foolyou flu is capable of being transmitted with or without contact. Second, the illness is due to a microorganism. Third, this minute thing can cause an infection, which can lead to a lot of pain and maybe even death. Infection is the state or condition in which the body, or a part of it, is invaded by a pathogenic agent (microorganism or virus), which, under favorable conditions, multiplies and produces injurious effects. The symptoms of infection are pain, heat, redness, swelling, and disordered function. These symptoms are pretty much what you are experiencing with Foolyou flu—sore throat, headache, nausea, and perhaps vomiting.

What belief symptom is operating here? *The belief that illness is something that can be caught!* It is spread by virulent little organisms you can't see. You don't even have to be near the sick person to catch them! Once you catch these organisms, they cause an infection, and you can get very sick or maybe even die. If I believed that to be true, I would also be scared.

But, what really happened? You were in a state of balance, without dis-ease, when you first became aware of the epidemic of Foolyou flu going around. Remember, thoughts are energy and must be in a constant stare of balance. When you first heard about Foolyou flu, you started thinking about it. When you heard about the symptoms, how terribly ill you get, and how long it takes to recover, you became fearful. If we are experiencing fear, we are out of balance. When we are out of balance, the body tries to correct itself by creating that on which we focus our attention. The rest was easy. Your unconscious mind and body created that which you feared—Foolyou flu. Since you feared it, you spent a lot of time and energy repressing that fear, and, in doing so, you focused your unconscious mind on what you feared. Because you were focusing a lot of energy thinking about and fearing the flu, your body responded by doing the only thing it could do—to create Foolyou flu.

Lift your right hand up and look at it. How does it feel? Now start imagining that you have a pain in your little finger. Really concentrate on your little finger and the pain you feel in it. What happens? Your little finger starts to hurt. This is a simple explanation of what I am talking about. Of course, in this demonstration, you are causing the pain with the conscious mind. When we create an illness, it is usually the unconscious mind causing disease. What our conscious mind sees, thinks, or hears, our unconscious mind accepts as truth. It's the old adage: what we think is what we are.

How does being out of balance cause our dis-ease process? Balance simply means a state of equilibrium. Equilibrium is a state where contending forces are equal. Since all energy has a positive and negative force, to be balanced means that the positive and negative forces are equal and exist in a state of harmony. When we are in balance, we are able to experience ease, free from dis-ease. The terms *positive* and *negative* don't refer to good and bad energy, but simply to opposite forces.

We are prone to believe what we fear is bad, or we would not fear it. Not only do we feel it is bad, but, because we fear it, it must be powerful. If we fear it, we certainly do not want to look at it, so we repress it. We bury that fear so far down in our psyche that we forget we once feared it. Then we wonder why we get sick.

Remember, we are dealing with energy, and when we repress energy, we block it. The energy is no longer in balance and free to express itself. That which we repress, we must manifest. When we repress fear or any other emotion, that emotion has no choice but to manifest in our life in one form or another.

To manifest is to create or make real. When we are afraid of catching the Foolyou flu, we set ourselves up to ensure that we will create it. It can't work any other way. The energy we have repressed with our fear of illness must be released and expressed as something. As we fear something, as we push it away, we give it so much energy that we must draw it forth. Did we catch the Foolyou flu? No! Did we have to become ill? No! Did we do it to ourselves, either consciously or unconsciously? Yes!

Now that we are sick—how do we get well? If it you want to seek traditional medical attention for any dis-ease process, then that is what you must do. The use of Reiki will never interfere with any medical regimen. Reiki enhances anything you may be taking or doing to get well. If you use holistic tools to allow the body to heal, then Reiki is an important complementary tool.

As you read this book you are learning how to use the magnificent power and energy within you and combine it with the wonderful power around you to facilitate the healing of the body, mind, and emotions. Reiki is so much more than a healing system; it is a tool we use to strive to reach enlightenment, the highest form of balance. Reiki teaches us to be, to allow, to grow, and, most importantly, to unlock the door to allow us to recognize, feel, and connect to our inner Source.

I am often asked if Reiki is considered holy. Reiki has a divine nature or origin, but no more than you do. Reiki is you, as Source, manifesting as direct energy to re-establish balance in any person, situation, or emotion that is out of balance. Every person, place, or thing in our world is energy and, as such, should be honored and treated with respect. This means honoring and respecting people we do not particularly like. When you see someone you're not fond of, say to yourself, "The God in me recognizes and honors the God in you." As you make a habit of doing this, you will notice a subtle shift in your perception of people.

Should you be in awe of Reiki? No more than you are in awe of yourself. Reiki receives its power from Source, the same power residing within you. You are Source. When you treat Reiki with respect, you are also treating yourself with respect. If you are in the habit of asking for guidance whenever you attempt to help people, then do so when practicing Reiki. If this is not your habit, Reiki works just as well. There are many Reiki masters who say that you should pray before starting a healing. This is fine if it is your preference. Just remember that prayer does not start the Reiki flow. Your intention to use Reiki energy is what starts the flow.

Over the years, the practice of Reiki has almost developed into a religion, or holy form of healing, while loudly proclaiming that it isn't. Reiki is a wonderful, creative, magical energy, just as you are a wonderful, creative, magical Source of that energy. Is it of divine Source? Of course, but so is everything else in this universe.

Reiki is meant to be used, and since it is a direct manifestation of Source, its uses are unlimited. Have fun with it, play with it, experiment with it, and know it is there to do whatever you desire, as is the whole of creation.

REVIEW

- Our consciousness is divided into three parts: the conscious, unconscious, and supraconscious minds. We can know what is in our conscious mind, because most of the time we know what we are thinking. Our unconscious mind is often shrouded in secrecy. Here we bury our fears and failures; here we are judge and jury to our actions; here we learn to have self-doubts and low self-esteem. It is often this forgotten morass of emotions that creates the life we are living. Our supraconscious mind is often referred to as our spiritual self.

- Reiki works on all three levels of consciousness. By allowing us to access and accept all that is buried in our unconscious mind, Reiki gives us the opportunity to heal ourselves. We can never be cured until the unconscious mind is rid of the fears and emotions that created dis-ease in the first place.

- Our body takes direction from the mind. Unfortunately our body does not know if the mind is telling the truth or not. What the mind says to create, we do. All too often the order is coming from the unconscious mind, and we are creating that which we fear the most. Since all of this is occurring below our level of consciousness, we really do not know how we get sick. Reiki opens the door so we can consciously become aware of the cause of our problems. In this way we can integrate this fear and release it, thereby restoring balance and health. Reiki teaches how to consciously, consistently create our lives.

Psychological causes of dis-ease

Our body acts upon the commands of our conscious or unconscious mind to create our dis-ease processes. These commands are often the result of emotions we are unaware of or that we have repressed deep into our unconscious mind. Listed below are some of the common dis-ease processes and the emotions related to them.

Accidents: anger, frustration, rebellion.
Anorexia/Bulimia: self-hate, denial of life nourishment, not
    feeling good enough.
Asthma: smothering-love, guilt complex, inferiority complex.
Back problems: uptightness.
Back pain:
    upper—not feeling supported emotionally, needing support.
    middle—guilt.
    lower—burnout, worrying about money.
Bladder: release of pressure.

Blood: life-force, vitality.

Bones: firmness, fulfillment of desires.

Burns, boils, fevers, sores, swellings: anger.

Cancer: deep resentment, distrust, self-pity, hopelessness, helplessness.

Colon: constipation is an inability to let go, diarrhea is a fear of holding.

Ears: obedience, not accepting what is said.

    earaches—anger.

    deafness—refusal to hear.

Feet: understanding, steadfastness, rooted, humility, submissiveness.

Fingernails and Toenails: aggression.

Gallbladder: aggression.

Genitals: sexuality or rejecting sexuality, self worth, sexual prowess, denial of female worth, sexual guilt, fear of sex.

Gums: confidence.

Hair: freedom, power.

Hands: comprehension, ability to act, holding on too tightly to money or relationships.

Head: fear of how we appear to others, self loathing.

Headaches: invalidation of self.

Heart: ability to love, emotion, denial of self, love, and joy.

Kidneys: partnership.

Knees: humility, submissiveness, inflexibility, pride, ego, stubbornness, fear of change.

Large Intestine: greed, the unconscious.

Limbs: mobility, flexibility, activity.

Liver: discrimination, philosophy, religion.

Lungs: contact, communication, freedom, denial of life, inferiority.

Migraines: anger, perfection, frustration.

Mouth: readiness to accept.

Muscles: mobility, flexibility, and activity.

Neck: fear, anxiety, flexibility issues.

Nose: power, pride, sexuality.

Overweight: needing protection, security issues.

Pain: guilt seeking punishment.

Penis: power.

Sinus: irritated by someone.

Skin: contact, tenderness.

Small intestine: processing, analysis.

Stiffness: inflexible, resistance to change

Stomach: feelings, receptivity.

Strokes: lack of joy, negative thinking, fear.

Teeth: aggression, vitality.

Throat: fear, anxiety, fear of change, anger, frustration, stifled creativity.

Tumors: inability to let go, not allowing healing of old wounds.

Ulcers: fear, lack of self-worth.

Vagina: self-surrender.

CHAPTER FIVE

Reiki I

Chinamen wear five buttons
only on their coats,
that they may keep in sight
something to remind them
of the five principal moral virtues
which Confucius recommended.
These are: Humility, Justice,
Order, Prudence, and Rectitude.

—Unknown

Reiki is universal energy, channeled through the practitioner's body and focused on an object. This energy properly aligns, or brings into balance, the energy within that object, usually for the purpose of healing. I am deliberately vague about the uses of Reiki because there is nothing in this world you cannot Reiki. I've used Reiki on flashlight batteries, on my car and computer (to keep them running), on plants and animals, to protect my house, to project energy into the future, to correct past experiences, to find a parking space, and for anything else that might have occurred to me. Reiki opens our awareness to the fact that we are Source, while establishing direct contact with universal Source. I would never think of placing a limit on that power!

I recently had a very bright, gifted, and powerful student, who, after completing her Reiki II training, decided she wanted to help souls who have passed on. She went to a local cemetery and started practicing Reiki on some graves. One was the grave of a young man apparently killed in the Vietnam war. As she was working on his grave, she distinctly heard him say "Hi!" Needless to say, this completely freaked her out, and she ran screaming from the cemetery. I'm telling this story for two purposes: one, Reiki works anywhere; and two, don't use it unless you want it to work. In effect, this student made contact from beyond "the veil of death" and then left him hanging there. If you are doing any kind of energy work, then you must have a desire to make contact. It's like calling someone on the phone, and then after they answer, leaving them hanging on an open line. I encourage you to use Reiki anywhere or anytime you have the desire. Just don't be surprised when it works! Remember, when you acknowledge the Source within and combine it with universal Source, there is nothing that can't be accomplished.

How to use Reiki

Reiki I primarily teaches you self-healing methods. Anytime you are using your hands for Reiki, the fingers should be close together with the thumb tucked next to the hand, just as if your hand was in a mitten. This position keeps the energy in one area. If your fingers are spread, you weaken the energy exiting through your hand, because the energy is going from finger to finger, rather than being focused on the person or object you are healing. The palms are usually facing the body, unless this is uncomfortable, as it would be when working on your own back. After a while this will become a very comfortable hand position.

When you are using the hand positions on yourself or on an object, rest them there gently, with no exerted pressure. Unless you are a massage therapist, nurse, doctor, or minister, you cannot touch anyone's body. When working on others, your hands should be a half-inch to an inch above the body. If you feel the need to touch a client's body, be sure to get permission first. Touching can be construed as sexual harassment.

When both hands are resting on an object, with the intent to heal, Reiki energy is automatically activated and starts flowing. As soon as you take away your intention to heal, the energy stops. Your intention is the off and on switch for Reiki; otherwise it would be flowing out of your hands all the time. Although Reiki is inexhaustible, you are not! Traditionalists teach that "putting the hands on the body" turns the Reiki power on. I disagree, because if you had to lower your hands to start the flow, how could you do long-distance healing? Your intention is all that is ever necessary to start Reiki flowing. When you remove your intent, the flow stops.

After your attunements you will feel subtle differences in your body. As Reiki is flowing through you, it is also healing and aligning your body. Using Reiki should not drain your energy or make you sleepy or exhausted. If you are experiencing these symptoms, then you have a blockage, and you need to consult your Reiki master to check your energy flow. If you are having unpleasant side effects from practicing Reiki, perhaps you need to spend some time cleansing and clearing your energy field. Again, contact your Reiki master for specific techniques.

When we decide to learn Reiki, we are all at different physical, mental, and emotional levels. Although Reiki will work for anyone, sometimes we need help to learn how to remove some of our long-standing blockages. We are like a chimney and, at times, we need a chimney sweeper to get rid of the residue of our past experiences, thoughts, and habits. Consistent use of Reiki will remove these blockages.

When you place your hands above the client in a Reiki position, you may feel a number of different sensations—cold, hot, vibrating, trembling, tingling, static electricity, color, sound, or (very rarely) pain—flowing through your hands. Another common feeling is one of pins and needles, as if your fingers had gone to sleep. In theory, the sensations continue in that one position as long as the person being healed is pulling the energy from the healer. Although it may feel longer, the usual time spent in each position is three minutes or less. After three minutes you should go to another hand position. Usually the sensation ends, and the normal body warmth returns. This is your signal to move to the next position.

There are times when you feel your hands are glued to one position and the sensations seem to go on forever. Continue that position for about three minutes, and then gently move your hands to the next position. Obviously, more healing needs to done here, but that particular dis-ease did not develop overnight, and it will take more than one session for healing to occur. Also,

Reiki goes where it is needed, so even if you move your hands to another position, the previous affected area is still being treated. Some deeply rooted diseases may take several sessions to resolve.

We all succumb to a dis-ease process for different reasons and may not be ready to release our illness with just one or two treatments. Reiki works on all levels, including the emotional level (this is usually the level where we hold onto our illness), and with repeated Reiki sessions our unconscious reluctance to release our dis-ease process will be resolved. After you have worked with several clients, you will develop a sense of when it is time to change your hand position. Honor your intuition. Remember, there is no right or wrong way. Only do what feels comfortable to you.

The exception is when the client, on any level, refuses the Reiki treatment. Refusing effectively blocks the energy from entering his or her energy field. All people are free to determine if they want to be healed or not, and as a practitioner you must respect their wishes.

Reiki was originally taught without hand positions. Mrs. Takata founded the hand positions. Hand positions are valuable, because they divide the body into treatable sections, so you are basically treating the head, front torso, back torso, and extremities in logical sequence. It is also easier for the practitioner to concentrate on certain segments rather than the whole body.

Since the practitioner is stationary for long periods of time while allowing the flow of the Reiki healing energy, the use of hand positions gives the practitioner an opportunity to change positions and move around the client.

Psychologically it feels better to the practitioner to concentrate on certain segments. We feel we are accomplishing more by working on one segment at a time rather than trying to treat the whole body at once. Using the hand positions breaks the task down into do-able pieces. And the client feels better when he or she can experience the healing energy in a certain logical progression over his or her body.

Mrs. Takata was very wise in creating the hand positions. The only difference in my approach is that I teach there is no right or wrong way or order in the application of the hand positions. If you forget a position or feel an urge to change or modify a position, *always follow your intuition or urges*. Trusting your intuition is always more appropriate for you than anything anyone can teach you.

Hand Positions

All photographed hand positions show a Reiki practitioner performing a healing treatment. If the self-healing position is different, it is pictured alongside the healing position. Self-healing should be a comfortable, relaxing experience. A lot of practitioners self-heal right before going to sleep. If you start a session and fall asleep, that's fine. Reiki works as long as the intention is there. If you don't remove your intention until morning, then you receive an all-night healing session. What a wonderful experience! Remember, if any of these positions feel uncomfortable, or for some reason you cannot physically put your hands in

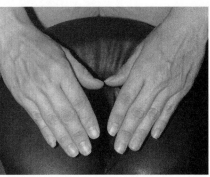

Hand Position

the position, modify it to fit your needs. I promise you, there will be no quiz!

Some masters teach that one hand is positive and one hand is negative and the hands have to be placed appropriately or the energy will not flow correctly. This is not correct. When Reiki exits the hands, it is whole, balanced energy. As a matter of fact, you can allow Reiki energy to flow using just one hand. I often do this while I am driving and see an accident or someone or something along the road that I feel needs Reiki energy. I keep one hand on the steering wheel and beam the energy out at them with my other hand.

Position 1 (Head Position 1)

In the first position, the hands are gently placed over the face, covering the forehead, eyes, cheeks, and jaw. If you are using this position on yourself, the palms are facing you, with the fingers pointing up to the forehead; the hands are side by side. If you are treating someone else, the palms are still toward the face, but the fingers are pointing to the chin, since you are standing at the crown. Remember to leave

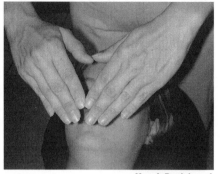

Head Position I

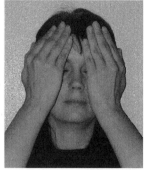

Self-Healing

room for the nose. If the nose is completely covered by your hands, the flow of the energy could interfere with breathing.

This position covers the eyes, sinuses, brain, and both halves of the face. It balances the two halves of the brain, opens the sinuses, and relaxes the mind. It is used for headaches, sinusitis, sinus congestion, teeth and jaw problems, eye problems, emotional and stress problems, and establishing a sense of calmness and peace.

Position 2 (Head Position 2)

In position two, the palms are slightly above each ear, with the fingers pointing to the forehead. Keep the hands right on the hairline.

This position covers the ears, facial muscles, nerves, cheeks, and jaw joints. It balances the two halves of the brain (emotion and reason). It is useful in case of stress or difficulty in learn-

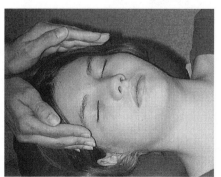

Head Position 2

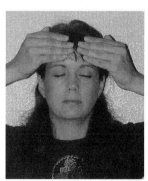

Self-Healing

ing, lack of concentration, and whenever there is an emotional imbalance. Colds, headaches, TMJ, grinding of teeth, molar problems, ear and hearing problems, as well as tension, are relieved using this position. It establishes a feeling of relaxation.

Position 3 (Head Position 3)

The hands cup the back of the head, effectively covering the whole back of the head. This position covers the reflex zones for the main chakras (energy centers) one through four—the back of the brain, the beginning of the spinal cord (affecting the large intestine and gall bladder), the medulla oblongata, brain stem, cerebellum, and pons. This position also stimulates the pineal gland. The pineal gland is the center of your spiritual being. Awakening or stimulating this gland allows access to our spiritual self.

This position is used for relaxation, headache, eye diseases, colds, abdominal complaints, anxiety, asthma, hyperventilation, circulatory complaints, and trigeminal and eighth facial nerve disorders. It is also good for sneezing, nausea, and brain stem problems, including blackouts, seizures, hearing loss, balance, and loss of coordination of the voluntary muscle movements, as well as fine voluntary movements, such as writing, dressing, and eating.

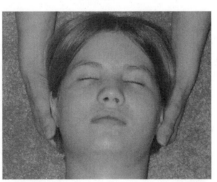

Self-Healing   **Head Position 3**

Position 4 (Head Position 4)

The palms are placed on each side of the jaw, with the fingers curving and meeting under the chin. For self-healing the hands are placed on the neck with the wrists together, palms embracing the neck, and the fingertips pointing toward each ear.

This position covers the bottom of the ear, throat, larynx, vocal cords, and lymph nodes. It is used for equilibrium problems, loss of hearing, metabolic disease, weight problems, anorexia, stuttering, anxiety, palpitation, poor posture, blood pressure problems, sore throat, hoarseness, ton-

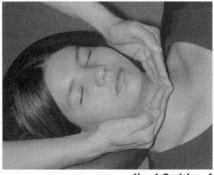

Head Position 4

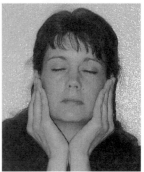

Self-Healing

sillitis, insecurity, aggressive behavioral problems, and chronic tension in the legs, pelvic area, and shoulder muscles.

Position 5 (Front Position 1)

The hands are placed above and across the breasts, with the fingertips pointing at each other. The fingertips can be lightly touching or not touching at all.

This position covers the parathyroid, thyroid, trachea, thymus, internal and external jugular vein, arch of the aorta, superior vena cava, vagus nerve, lungs, and heart.

It is used for weight problems, breathing and swallowing problems, immune disorders, wheezing, convulsions, muscle cramps, urinary frequency, mood changes, motor and sensory problems, asthma, and high blood pressure.

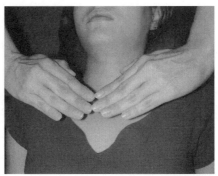

Front Position I

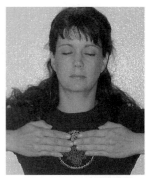

Self-Healing

Position 6 (Front Position 2)

The hands are placed on the lower rib cage, under the breasts and over the heart, one hand slightly in front of the other. In self-healing they are in the same position as in Position 5, only lower on the body.

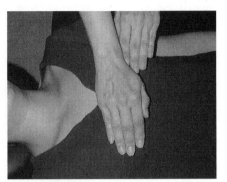

This position covers the heart, liver, spleen, gallbladder, pancreas, and part of the stomach. It is used for diabetes, clotting problems, white blood cell problems, digestion problems, cirrhosis of the liver, excessive bleeding problems, heart diseases, circulatory problems, and high blood pressure.

Self-Healing

Front Position 2

Position 7 (Front Position 3)

The hands are placed over the middle of the abdomen, one hand slightly in front of the other. I use the belly button as a guide. In self-healing the hands are in the same position as position 6, only lower on the body.

This position covers the stomach, pylorus, duodenum, and small and large intestine. It is used for treating ulcers (acid secretion is controlled by the pylorus), digestion problems, constipation, malabsorption of foods, bowel contrictions, bowel adhesions, nausea, diarrhea, parasite infections, and upset stomachs.

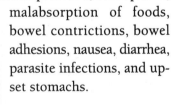

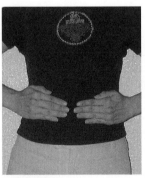

Self-Healing

Front Position 3

Position 8 (Front Position 4)

The hands are pointed downward, in a V-shape over the pelvic bone and lower abdomen. In self-healing the fingertips form a V above the pelvic ridge.

This position covers the reproductive organs, appendix, bladder, rectum, and sigmoid colon. It is used for menstrual pain, prostrate problems, ovulation problems, pregnancy, frequency of urination, bladder problems, constipation, sexual problems, weight problems, allergies, diseases of the urogenital system, and diseases or problems with the immune system.

Front Position 4

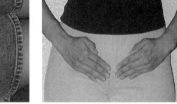
Self-Healing

Position 9 (Back Position 1)

The hands are placed on each shoulder, palms toward the body, fingers toward the back, effectively grabbing your shoulders in self-healing. When working on someone else, the hands are placed between the shoulder blades, with one hand slightly in front of the other. It is the opposite position of number 5.

This position covers the shoulder blades, spinal cord, and long voluntary muscles of movement. It is used for muscle aches, weakness, headaches, tension in the muscles, TMJ, and muscle spasms.

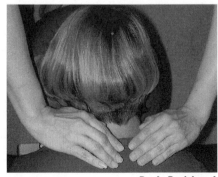
Back Position I

Self-Healing

Position 10 (Back Position 2)

The hands are placed just under the shoulder blades, opposite position 6. This position covers the lungs and adrenal glands. It is used for respiratory problems, asthma, and fluid on the lungs. The adrenal glands store and release dopamine, norepinepherine,

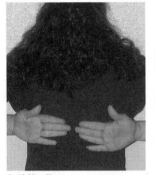

Self-Healing

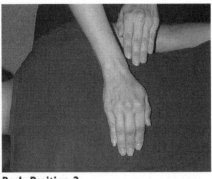

Back Position 2

and epinephrine. These control dilation and constriction of the arteries and veins and increase heart activity. They also produce the adrenocortical hormones (cortisol and cortisone), which are important in carbohydrate, water, muscle, bone, central nervous system, gastrointestinal, cardiovascular, and hematological metabolism. They are also anti-inflammatory agents. This is a major area for weight loss, fatigue, hypertension, hypotension, and mental changes.

Position 11 (Back Position 3)

The hands are placed in the middle of the back, above the flare of the hips, opposite position 7. This position covers the lumbar ver-

Self-Healing

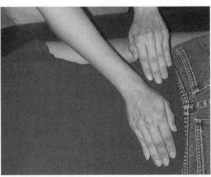

Back Position 3

tebrae and kidneys. It is used for mid-back sprains, aches and pains, kidney problems, water retention, blood in the urine, cloudy urine, foul-smelling urine, and detoxification.

Position 12 (Back Position 4)

The hands are placed in a V-formation, covering the sacrum with the point of the V directed toward the feet, opposite position 8. This position covers the sacrum, coccyx, and sciatic nerve. It is used for foot and leg movement problems, foot drop, pain and tingling in lower leg and

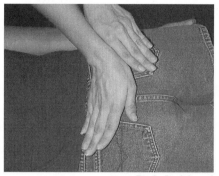

Back Position 4

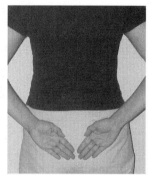

Self-Healing

foot, bedsores, rotation of the hips, fissures, digestive problems, and diseases of the urogenital system.

The feet and leg positions are usually used if the client has problems in these areas. Basically, you treat the hip, knee and ankle joints, and the bottom of the feet. The hand positions are as in the photos.

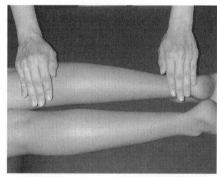

Leg Position

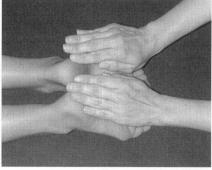

Foot Position

Helpful hint: I am more comfortable lying down when I do a treatment on myself, and I advise you to do the same. Reiki can be given in any position, but why not be comfortable doing it? When I am doing my back positions, I bring my knees up and plant my feet on the bed, thus relieving any back strain.

Reiki is tapping into the universal power source, and there is absolutely nothing this power cannot accomplish. This stated, I will also tell you to never, never, never play doctor, either with yourself or with clients or any students. The urge is *almost* irresistible!

I have been a registered nurse since 1965 and was fully entrenched in traditional medicine. I am now completely holistic. This does not mean that if I am in a terrible accident I will refuse the life-saving support modern medicine offers! It is great for keeping a person alive so that the body has time to heal itself, especially after a life-threatening accident. This wonderful, complicated body of ours was created with an innate ability to heal itself, and Reiki is part of this creation, coded in our DNA. Over the centuries, as we turned outward seeking medical assistance, we consequently have lost this ability and knowledge to heal ourselves. We have been taught to give our power away to doctors and the medical community.

With Reiki, we are reclaiming and taking our power back. So, in essence I am not teaching you anything you don't already know on some level. I am here to help you to remember and to attune your body to use this knowledge. Each one of us is a marvelous being, created with the knowledge of maintaining and sustaining ourselves in perfect health. Because centuries have passed since we used this knowledge to heal others and ourselves, our vibrational fields have changed and lowered. We need the attunements to synchronize our vibrational field with the vibrational field and force of Source.

Once you are attuned and realize just what a fantastic gift Reiki is, you might want to cure the world. This is fine and part of the process, but you must never play doctor. If you are under a doctor's care and taking any prescriptions, do not abandon the plan of treatment you are following. Do your Reiki, and let your inner voice be your guide. Always consult your physician before suspending or stopping any medications or plan of treatment. Some medications must be weaned from the body or you will create havoc with your sensitive endocrine and hormonal systems.

Since most of our clients are ill, many of them will be taking medications. Do your healing session and offer no advice on what they should or should not be taking. You do not know their whole medical history (nor do you want to), and you certainly do not want the responsibility of counseling anyone to stop taking their medication. There might be nasty legal ramifications if you do.

Everyone will eventually find his or her own path, in time. Our society is dependent on the quick fix, the pop-a-pill mentality. We forget it takes time to get sick and the opposite is always true—it takes time to get well. Do not try to rush the healing sessions or the healing process. Sometimes our bodies, minds, and emotions require the enforced confinement of an illness to readjust and realign to our modern, hectic lifestyle. Take time to heal and enjoy the process.

Remember, all dis-ease is created on several levels. When you are using Reiki to cure the body, its energy must work through and balance the other levels involved, or the cure will not be a long-term one. The habit of rushing is one of the reasons clients often have a return of symptoms or develop a new dis-ease process.

The physical manifestation of dis-ease, in order to be cleared properly, must be released from all the other realms that participated in creating the disorder in the first place. We are dealing with a complex organism that contains a physical, mental, and emotional body, along with seven outer, or ethereal, bodies.

Our dis-ease process usually starts on an external energy plane and is manifested in the body to get our attention. We must do whatever is necessary to put the physical body back in balance, or ease. Dis-ease is not a malfunction of the body; it is simply a symptom and warning that our body is out of balance. If we continue to ignore the warning, the body creates different and progressively more life-threatening states of dis-ease. Without resolution, this process usually ends in death. The body can be restored to ease in several ways:

1. Reiki I practitioners can perform repeated Reiki healing sessions, even after the symptoms appear to have disappeared, in order to stabilize all the levels of energy.

2. Reiki II practitioners can use the symbols to access the mental, emotional, and physical aspects of the body.

3. Reiki masters can work in the seven outer bodies to release blockages before they manifest in the body.

You should give your body time to get used to the different energy fields in which you are working and living, self-treat daily, and then do what feels right for you.

Once you have absorbed this knowledge and mastered the skills shown here, you are ready for your attunement. After this, go in peace. I thank you for choosing me as your Reiki master. We have established an unbreakable bond, and I am always here for you.

Your Reiki I Attunement

When you feel ready for your attunement, sit in a quiet room on a straight-backed chair with your arms and hands comfortably in front of you. Take a deep breath and relax. If you have the Reiki video, put the cassette in now. You will feel subtle changes in the energy around you. It is often beneficial before the attunement process to have read the attunement steps so you will be familiar with what is happening during the video. This will remove any fears you may have about the attunement process.

1. I start in front of you, channeling the energy and directing it to your whole body.

2. I walk around your left side and put my hand on your right shoulder.

3. I work above your crown.

4. I put my hands on your crown.

5. I put my hands on the back of your head.

6. I put my hands on both shoulders.

7. I put my hands directly over your heart.

8. I walk around to your right side and put one hand on your forehead and one hand on the back of your head. You may feel your third eye opening.

9. I walk to the front of you and put your hands together, palm to palm.

10. I hold your fingertips with my hand.

11. I readjust and hold your fingertips with my hand.

12. I angle your fingertips and point to your heart, forehead, and crown. You will feel me blowing my breath into these areas.

13. I lay your hands in your lap.

14. I walk to your back and ground you.

15. I walk around to the front, and you will feel a motion in the energy.

16. When all is quiet, open your eyes.

Place your hands in front of you, one on top and one on bottom. Separate them six to twelve inches. Now say to yourself, "It is my intent to use Reiki." You will feel the energy flowing between your hands. If someone placed their hand between your hands, you would feel their hands and they would feel your energy.

Remember, your energy field is changed by this attunement. Some people experience a detoxification process after the attunement. This may resemble a light case of the flu. You may experience some nausea, diarrhea, or stomach upset. Avoid all caffeine and drink lots of water, and use your Reiki. Pamper yourself. Give yourself a little gift of rest and relaxation. This process never lasts more than a few days. Put your hands on your body, have the intent to use Reiki, and conduct a healing session on yourself.

I have a student (he has since become a master) who, after his first attunement, was given the same advice about no caffeine, drinking lots of water, and taking care of himself. He chose to ignore my advice. He went home and had several cups of coffee. He was still washing walls at four in the morning! Believe me, he took good care of himself after his Reiki II and Masters attunements.

People often ask me if Reiki I really works. I'll answer that with another story. A young man with advanced throat cancer came to one of our Reiki exchange nights. He was obviously very sick and in a lot of pain during the first part of the evening. When it came time to perform the Reiki treatments, I chose him as my client. As I was concentrating on his healing, I noticed a dimming of all of the lights in the room. I looked around and saw that all the other practitioners had finished their healing sessions and had formed a circle around us. They were all beaming energy at us. There was so much focused energy in that room that it affected the lights! After the session, this young man whispered to me that in his hurry to get to the meeting, he had forgotten to take his pain medication. He said it didn't matter, because now he was pain-free for the first time in years.

I taught him Reiki I, and he received his first attunement. He didn't attend any Reiki exchange sessions for several months. One evening I received a call from him. He was speaking in a normal voice on the phone and stated that he was in remission, was pain-free, and that his hair was even starting to grow back. He said, "Thank you, Barb. I want you to know Reiki is alive and well."

While it is true that we, as a group, started the healing process, it was his own self-work with Reiki I that cured his cancer. Does Reiki I work? Sure it does.

I teach that practicing Reiki is an act of love to our fellow humans, our planet, our universe, and ourselves. I live by this little verse: "All acts that are not acts of perfect love are acts of self-denial, and therein lies our pain."

Since I, for one, do not relish living in pain, I try to make everything I do an act of perfect love, therefore nourishing first myself, then my own little world, and finally expanding to the whole universe. Living, practicing, and teaching Reiki is an act of perfect love. Congratulations, you are now a first degree Reiki practitioner.

SUMMARY

Reiki I is your introduction to the awesome world of Reiki. Here, often for the first time, you experience the flow of universal life force energy entering and flowing through your body. You have been instructed in the hand positions used during a healing session and, I hope, you have practiced these positions.

Reiki I is used for self-healing and the healing of anyone physically present. Since everything consists of energy, Reiki works on animate and inanimate objects alike. Reiki I teaches you to balance the energy of anything you can touch in your world.

Your attunement has changed your world by changing the vibrational force surrounding your body. Your third eye was opened, and you may experience life just a little brighter. Your dreams may be more vivid, and your energy level should be increased. Your crown and heart have been opened, and a pathway has been established for the flow of energy into your crown, through your heart, and out your hands.

With the opening of your heart, you may experience forgiveness for those who have harmed you. You may also have learned to love and honor yourself. Your body has experienced massive changes and will continue to change for some time. Be good to yourself, pamper yourself, and, most importantly, use Reiki on yourself.

CHAPTER SIX

Reiki II

Love means an exchange of
service for service—
and God's law demands that service given
must equal service rendered.

—Walter Russell, *The Divine Iliad*

Congratulations on deciding to continue your Reiki education. With the completion of your first degree Reiki training and attunement, the primary power-receiving channels have been opened, affecting the crown, heart, and palm areas. This opening establishes a pathway for the flow of the energy from the crown, to the heart, and out the hands. This pathway allows the Reiki energy to flow freely from and through you and helps your body to adapt to the flow. Your heart has been opened, and you are now aware of the energy housed in your own body and mind. You will feel an increase in your psychic abilities due to the opening of your third eye. Perhaps your dreams are more vivid or life has just taken on a different flavor. You are now vibrating at a higher frequency, and your body should be attuned to it. You have practiced self-healing to experience what it feels like to be in balance and at one within yourself. You may have noticed that some of your perceptions have changed, and you are more at peace with yourself. This is what comes from living in balance.

Second degree Reiki boosts the power connection and teaches you to perform Reiki healing sessions on others as well as to heal at a distance. You will now learn to send Reiki anywhere you choose, to work and manipulate the timeline, to correct past creations, and to create positive situations in your future. Once you have received your Reiki II attunement, you will have the knowledge and ability to open a business, treat clients, and make money doing so. You are a true Reiki practitioner and can start making this your life's work, if you so choose.

I would like to talk a little bit about Reiki and money. Spiritual communities appear almost schizophrenic about discussing money. One extreme is the people who believe that in order to be spiritual you must disregard money and live a life of near-poverty. They feel money is somehow dirty and corrupts you spiritually. I heartily disagree. Money allows you to be very spiritual. With money you can live in a nice house, dress well, be comfortable, and be an example to others. It is easier to give and be generous to others when you have enough money to do so. It is difficult to learn anything when you are hungry, when you have no place to sleep, when you are worried about feeding yourself or your family, or when your bills are so overwhelming you can think of nothing else.

On the other side of the coin is the Reiki master who charges thousands of dollars for classes. For justification, this person refers back to part of Dr. Usui's legend. I did not include this segment in my history of Reiki, because I wanted to address it here.

After his meeting with the abbot of the monastery, Dr. Usui decided to go to the slums of the city and to live there and heal the people. He thought that if anyone needed healing, these poor people of the slums did. He sent several of these young men to the monastery to be taught Reiki and become practitioners. They were then sent out into the city to practice healing. Thus he endowed each practitioner with the power to earn his living.

Eventually he began to notice familiar faces as he walked through the slums. He was shocked to realize that these were some of the young men he had sent to the monastery for Reiki training. They had returned to the slums, because they thought that earning a living by performing Reiki treatments was more difficult than going out and begging each day.

Dr. Usui realized that by his giving away Reiki so freely, the beggars had developed no appreciation for the wonderful gift he gave them. He determined never again to give Reiki to anyone who did not appreciate it.

Traditional Reiki masters used this story to set very high prices for their Reiki classes. Some still charge up to $10,000 for the Reiki Master training. When I questioned this practice by stating that, at those prices, only the rich could become practitioners, I was told that Reiki was not for everyone, and that one had to have a certain level of intelligence to learn Reiki. In other words, this master was equating being poor with being stupid. Again, I heartily disagree, and this is one of my driving reasons behind this book.

What Dr. Usui was referring to is the human tendency to attach little or no value to something that is given to us. I am not talking about personal gifts. I am talking about the feeling that if the teacher does not value what is being taught, why should I? I know I personally do not place as high a value on something I am given as I do on something I have worked for.

Therefore, there must be a fair exchange for services. This can range anywhere from charging for your services and classes to bartering for them. The key word here is fair. Reiki has immense value, and if we give it away we do an injustice to Reiki. I perform a huge amount of free long-distance-healing; this is my-payback to the universe. But I always charge for my classes. Sometimes my charge is a car wash or some other service depending on the financial position of the student. I never refuse to teach anyone who does not have the money to pay, I just work out some other exchange of services. Just think of the cost of going to a traditional doctor, being admitted to the hospital, or getting a prescription. Do you even think of not paying for any of these services? So, why should your Reiki be free?

As a Reiki II practitioner you should start charging for your healing sessions. This places value on the service you are providing and also creates the thought in the client's mind that they are contributing to their own wellness. How often have you heard people say about their doctors, "He sure is expensive, but he's worth it."?

When most people first become second-level practitioners, they are so thrilled with what they have learned that they run around performing healing sessions for anyone who will lie still.

At this stage, even the pets run scared! This is fine, but there comes a time when they run out of friends and family and must look elsewhere for clients. This is usually when they begin to consider charging for the service.

Remember, it is through you that Source provides the energy for the healing. This is at least as valuable as a visit to a doctor's office. After we have practiced on family and friends, we may find that they do not value our services as much as we do. Why? Because we have not had an honest exchange for services, and they unconsciously devalue our services. I have found that when I work on family or friends for free, they are often inconsiderate of my time and efforts and feel they are doing me a favor by letting me practice on them. Neither I nor any other practitioner needs practice that badly.

If the Reiki I attunement opens us to the Source energy, the second-degree Reiki attunement greatly empowers that energy. Your first attunement began when the energy entered and changed the level of energy within your body. The second attunement builds upon this change and dramatically adds to these energy changes.

The Reiki I attunement created a pathway from your crown to your heart and opened your third eye, your crown, and your heart. The Reiki II attunement completes the pathway from your crown to your heart by creating the pathway out of your hands. This energy pathway is now complete. Part of the attunement is to slap the symbols into your hands, thereby sealing Reiki in you forever. It's a wonderful experience.

As your attunement changes your vibrational force, you may experience some inner changes. These may affect the foods you choose to eat, your attitudes toward life and experiences, and your general outlook. You may also experience some detox symptoms, such as diarrhea and stomach upset. If so, drink lots of water, avoid caffeine, and eat a bland diet for a couple of days. Put your hands on yourself to stabilize the vibrational changes. Traditional Reiki teaches it takes twenty-one days to go through the detox period and stabilize your vibrational field. I have not experienced it taking that long, and neither have any of my students. In my experience everything, including the physical symptoms, stabilizes within a couple of days. The vibrational field continues to change as you practice Reiki, and you will continuously notice changes in your energy flow, thoughts, actions, and responses. These changes can cause symptoms for up to six months.

When my agent received the manuscript for this book, she had no idea what Reiki was or how it worked. She read the manuscript and liked it. I sent her the Reiki I attunement video, and she received her first attunement.

Shortly after her attunement, she developed a multitude of abdominal symptoms. Having no idea what was occurring, she went to doctor after doctor and had a lot of expensive lab tests. She still did not have a medical diagnosis. This lasted for six months! Of course, she was very concerned with what was occurring within her body. After six months, the symptoms stopped.

She was actually experiencing the release of some long-held, powerful, unconscious feelings and beliefs. Once these were released, her symptoms stopped.

Reiki II Symbols

Reiki symbols have been kept in the strictest confidence for generations. They were never printed or copied, and students weren't allowed to show them to anyone. It was through this practice of secrecy that some aspects of Reiki became lost. Imagine, if you can, being a student in Mrs. Takata's class. You are studying Reiki, and when you leave class, all your notes and notebooks stay in the class or are destroyed. Time passes, and you are teaching your own Reiki classes. Suddenly, you can't recall if a symbol was drawn one way or the other. You certainly don't want to mislead your students, so you omit teaching the areas where you have doubts. Or worse, you teach it the way you feel it should be, even if you're hazy on all the details.

Although these omissions were completely unintentional, some pertinent Reiki information was lost. For example, I have seen many variations of the symbols. Which ones are correct? Do all of them work? Of course they do because it is the intent to use the symbol correctly that enhances the Reiki power. How did we get so many variations of the symbols if everyone was teaching the same symbol? Because people forgot and drew the symbol as best they could.

This lost knowledge is coming back to us through our Reiki guides. My Reiki guides are the source of much of the information in this book. There is a lot of new information coming in, so if you come in contact with something new or different, run it through your feelings and do what you believe is right for you. You are dealing with the highest Source, so trust that Source and your own intuitive powers.

As you begin to learn these symbols, remember that they are written in Japanese and are intended to transmit a picture. The writing and the lines are very graceful, and the symbols are things of beauty. But they are only symbols; their power comes from Source and our intent to utilize them. On their own they have no power and therefore do not have to be kept hidden. Do not be afraid of these symbols; use them freely, whenever and wherever, you feel the need to do so. If someone who has not studied Reiki came upon these symbols, they would have no idea what they were or how to use them. Therefore, for that person, these symbols would have no power.

An interesting thing happened to my agent over twenty years ago. While doing research about an illness, she stumbled across a Japanese book that pictured many of the Reiki symbols. Intuitively she knew that these symbols were important to her and contained answers to her questions, but she had no way to unlock the symbols and access the knowledge. She formed the intent to someday unlock the secret of these symbols. She asked for guidance to help her understand what the symbols meant and how she could use them. Twenty years later, *Self-Healing Reiki* landed on her desk. She feels that asking for help to understand the symbols in the past influenced my selection of her as my agent. In this way she was introduced to Reiki and the meaning of the Reiki symbols. "It only took twenty years!" she says.

The first symbol is **Cho-Ku-Rei** (*cho-coo-ray*). It is what I call the *light switch* or *opener*. Many Reiki practitioners draw little Cho-Ku-Rei symbols in their palms before starting a healing session to turn on the healing energy. In actuality, their intent to use Reiki turns on the energy, and the drawing of the symbol is but a physical action to reinforce their intention. If it feels good to draw the symbols on your hands, do so. Just remember, it is not necessary to draw the symbols.

Cho-Ku-Rei works on the physical plane and "sets" the energy. It serves to increase the power of any other symbol you may use, so I encourage you to use it while performing a healing session. When you add Cho-Ku-Rei to any work you're doing, the energy level is greatly boosted.

By visualizing the Cho-Ku-Rei symbol, your ability to access the energy is increased many times. It should be used any time you are dealing with energy, including driving down the road and wanting to clear traffic from your path. It's a simple matter to Cho-Ku-Rei the cars in front of you so they mysteriously decide to turn off the road. Try it; it works. It's also wonderful for finding a parking space.

I was once in the direct line of an out-of-control car and knew it was going to slam into me. I started sending the Cho-Ku-Rei at the approaching car like crazy, and it completely missed me. I actually saw the energy bump the car out of my way. You should have seen that driver's face!

Cho-Ku-Rei works on flashlights, car batteries, gas tanks, and anything and everything you can think of. The recipient does not have to be alive, as we know it, because everything in the universe is composed of energy. Reiki works to correct or balance the flow of energy in animate as well as inanimate objects.

Cho-Ku-Rei concentrates Reiki energy in one focused spot by the spiral shape of the symbol. The spiral or labyrinth shape swirls the energy and brings it to a fine focus wherever you are directing it to go. It is a very smooth, powerful symbol and is easily reversed if you wish to do so. Use it clockwise for increase and counterclockwise for decrease (it is the opposite for our friends in the southern hemisphere). Usually when you are working on a client you will use the symbol clockwise. The exception would be when dealing with a tumor or something you would like to remove from the body. In cases like this, use Cho-Ku-Rei counterclockwise to decrease or remove the object. Intent is paramount.

Sei-He-Kei (*say-he-kay*) is the second Reiki II symbol and is generally described as the emotional healer. All physical dis-ease has an emotional counterpart which must be addressed during the healing session. This is where Sei-He-Kei comes into play. It symbolizes Source and human coming together. As humans, when we attach feelings to a thought, we create an emotion. This emotion is often very powerful, making it difficult to deal with. Since thoughts are pure energy and Source is pure energy, Sei-He-Kei brings them together and balances the two energies.

The emotions we keep close to us and bury deep (and usually forget about) are always the painful, hurting emotions. Did you ever notice that when you experience joy you live it, and when you experience fear you bury it? Because we bury rather than deal with these emotions, they fester and grow out of proportion to the hurt that originally caused the pain. They are being ignored, and to remind us to deal with them they cause physical symptoms, which we label diseases.

For example, say your boss is constantly yelling at you for things you have or have not done. You know if you tell your boss what you're really thinking, you would be unemployed in the blink of an eye. So you swallow your unspoken words and accept the abuse the boss is handing out. Is it any wonder that many years later you develop cancer of the throat, ulcers, or any of the other illnesses associated with swallowing and the digestive tract? Your body is out of balance and is trying to tell you so by developing symptoms associated with the act that caused the imbalance.

Another example is an abusive spouse, who always belittles you in front of family or friends. You know if you talk back, or even defend yourself, it leads to a full-scale battle, and maybe even physical abuse. So you just remain quiet to preserve the peace or to avoid the embarrassment of a full-scale fight in public. Again, you have swallowed your emotion. It is no surprise that years down the road you are prone to develop throat cancer, ulcers, abdominal cancer, or any other dis-ease associated with swallowing or the digestive system.

A woman who is always being put down for being female often develops breast cancer or disease of the female reproductive system. Someone who is cold and uncaring, or tries to be, often develops disease of the heart or circulatory system (the heart being the center of love). I could go on and on, but I think you get the picture.

There is a saying, "As above, so below." Anger, frustration, fear, grief, and loneliness are more often the source of human disease than any bacteria, virus, or organic malfunction. The "above" is our emotional grasp of our actions, and the "below" is the unconscious, emotional punishment we order our bodies to carry out. Stated another way, when we have to swallow our anger for others, we turn that anger onto ourselves.

How often have you gotten mad at yourself when you did not respond to a situation as you later thought you should have? This internal anger miraculously changes to guilt in our psyche. Anger dissipates, but guilt can last forever. If we are guilty, we must be punished. What is our most popular way of punishing ourselves? You got it—physical dis-ease! The Sei-He-Kei will short-circuit this guilt process by bringing forward the emotions entwined with our dis-ease process and allowing us to deal with and release them.

Reiki is the key to consciousness healing that so many people have overlooked. Invoking Sei-He-Kei focuses the Reiki energy on the emotional body and intensifies its effects. It awakens the Source within, repatterns our thought processes, changes our vibrational field, and heals the mind-body connection through the subconscious. The symbol also cleanses negative energy, cleans out any blockages we may have, releases cravings, and changes our behavioral patterns. You can learn to use it consistently with wonderful results.

Using Sei-He-Kei in a healing session often uncaps these buried emotions, brings them to the surface, and allows us deal with them, thereby eliminating the emotional cause of our dis-ease. Once you reconnect with the pain of an old emotion and release it, it evaporates, leaving the way clear for the physical body to heal. Remember, we often manifest dis-ease to handle emotions we cannot deal with or forgot we had to deal with. Once we deal with the emotions, healing follows.

Hon-Sha-Ze-Sho-Nen (*hon-shaw-zee-show-nen*) is the third Reiki II symbol. It works in the spiritual plane. It is the symbol that transmits energy across distance, space, and time. This is the most powerful and complex of the Reiki II symbols. It works in the esoteric plane. It is used for long-distance healing as well as direct healing, to travel back and forth on the timeline, and to enter and work in the spiritual plane. It works together with the Sei-He-Kei, as often the emotional and spiritual aspects of ourselves are intimately entwined.

When we bring up our emotional traumas, Hon-Sha-Ze-Sho-Nen gives us the courage to release them, thereby healing the dis-ease process. This symbol truly allows us to suspend judgment on our past actions and reactions. In so doing, we forgive ourselves. When using Hon-Sha-Ze-Sho-Nen, we often experience a sense of peace, as if all is right in life and the world in general. We are spiritual animals, and working in this plane we often feel as if we have "come home."

Time is our way of measuring our existence, but in reality all we have is now. There is no past or future, only the present. Physics teaches that if time could be charted on a curve, and if you could extend the curve far enough, the past would meet the future. I like to think it does meet continuously, and we call this meeting the present. Acting on this theory, we can then easily access our past or our future. If we go to our past to resolve old traumas and release hidden emotions, we can then free ourselves of our self-sabotaging behavior. If we have an important event occurring at some future time, we can send Reiki energy to that point in time so, when we encounter the event, we will step into it with our extra bump of Reiki energy.

Soon after I became a Reiki master, I woke up one Saturday with a terrible pain on the right side of my neck. (Since I have been an R.N. for more years than I care to count, I knew I had an obstruction in my carotid artery, and the only cure was extensive, risky surgery.) I thought, "I really don't need this," and using my brand new knowledge, decided to go back in time to resolve the problem. I centered myself, drew the Hon-Sha-Ze-Sho-Nen in my mind while repeating the words, and asked to be transported back to the time before this clot was created. When I felt I had arrived at that point in time, I simply stated that the "Blood flows freely throughout my body without any obstructions." I again drew the Hon-Sha-Ze-Sho-Nen and asked to be brought back to the present. When I opened my eyes, I was completely pain-free and have not had a reoccurrence since.

It is just as simple to travel forward in time. If you have an important event coming up and you want to be sure it goes the way you desire, simply deposit energy to wait for you at the event. A new Reiki II practitioner lost her job right before she became a practitioner. After receiving her attunement, she decided to try to use the Reiki energy to find a job. She pictured the job she desired and drew the Cho-Ku-Rei to manifest that job for her. While looking in the paper, she found what she considered the perfect job. She called and set up an interview. While relaxing, she would draw the Hon-Sha-Ze-Sho-Nen in her mind, and then she would visualize herself at the interview. She included as many details as she knew and finished the visualization with her accepting the job. She drew another Hon-Sha-Ze-Sho-Nen to send the energy to the future interview.

When she walked into the interview, she felt the energy waiting for her. This was the best interview she ever had. She knew all the right responses and felt very confident. The interview was on a Wednesday, and they told her they would make their decision a week from Friday. They called her the following Monday, five days before they said they would make their decision, and offered her the job. She is very happy with her new job.

I'm not going to say I know how this works. After all, I still do not understand how the dots travel through air and appear on my television in the exact same order as the picture at the television studio. All I know for sure is that when I turn on my television,

I see a complete picture. The same logic applies to timeline healing. All I know for sure is that when I visualize and name the Hon-Sha-Ze-Sho-Nen symbol to access either the past or the future, it works. I don't know how, but I trust Reiki as much as I trust my television set to produce a picture every time I turn it on.

This is a wonderful tool and gift. Source would not have created this complex, exquisite body and then require us to go to an outside source for our maintenance and healing. Reiki is part of who and what we are. It's Source's gift to us, so we are able to maintain this body, in good health, for as long as we so desire. If that means we must travel back and forth in time, then we have the vehicle available to do that. I always say, "Don't look a gift time machine in the mouth!"

There are three symbols for Reiki II and two more for Reiki III. Although more symbols are becoming available every day, these are the only ones I personally use and teach. If you find another symbol that resonates to you, by all means, use it. Experiment with what is available, and do whatever your intuition leads you to do.

The Cho-Ku-Rei focuses on the physical body, the Sei-He-Kei addresses the emotional or unconscious body, and the Hon-Sha-Ze-Sho-Nen works in the spiritual plane. I use all three symbols in every healing session I do, even if I am not going to send any energy. Why? Because I feel each session should have the benefit of healing the physical, emotional, and spiritual aspects of the body.

You should memorize the symbols, which may take some time. I would suggest you draw them on paper to fix in your mind what they look like, and then practice drawing them in the air. Since there are many different versions of the symbols available, and I presume they all work, I do not put the emphasis on drawing them exactly as I have presented. If there was only one right way to draw the symbols, then a lot of us would be in trouble. If it is your intention to use any of the symbols and you suddenly go blank, don't panic. Just state your intention and the name of the symbol, if you remember it. If not, state what the symbol does, and Source will take care of the rest. Remember that you and Source are always working together, so if you forget something, stand aside and let Source take over.

Drawing the Reiki Symbols

Symbol 1: Cho-Ku-Rei

This is the light switch or opener. The Cho-Ku-Rei concentrates energy in one focused spot by the spiral shape of the symbol. It goes from a large arc to a small point, thereby swirling the energy and releasing it, similar to a laser light. In the northern hemisphere the symbol is drawn clockwise; in the southern hemisphere it is drawn counterclockwise.

To draw the Cho-Ku-Rei, start at the top of the page on the right side.

1. From right to left draw a straight line, about two inches long (line 1).

2. Then go straight down, north to south, about five inches long (line 2).

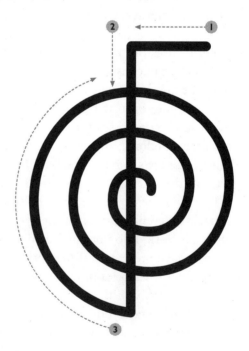

Cho-Ku-Rei

3. At the tip of the line start drawing a decreasing circle from left to right and up, with the line in the middle of the circle (line 3).

4. The outside of the circle is the largest. Inside the circle, decreasing in size, draw three more circles.

5. End with the tip of the last circle hooked around the straight line.

It is very helpful to have someone read the directions to you while you are drawing the symbols.

Symbol 2: Sei-He-Kei

The Sei-He-Kei is traditionally drawn for emotional healing. It is a good tool to delve into the subconscious and discover the reasons why we continue to sabotage ourselves in our everyday lives. We can use it to discover the emotional causes for physical disease and *how to release these emotions.*

I call the Sei-He-Kei the dragon symbol, because it resembles the head and neck of a dragon when completed. With that thought in mind, on a sheet of paper, starting slightly to the left of the middle, about two inches from the top:

1. Draw a line from right to left, angling downward, an inch long (1).

2. At the base point, angle the line back from left to right for an inch. These two lines should look like half of a diamond shaped sign (2).

3. Remember to connect all the lines, and come straight down for about three quarters of an inch (3).

4. The next part looks like half a square when finished. From right to left draw straight out for a half inch, then straight down for one inch, and then straight back for a half inch (4, 5, 6).

5. Sweep down from top to bottom with a slight curvature to the right. This is the neck part of the dragon (7).

6. Return to the top of the page.

7. Starting above and to the left of the symbol you have already drawn, without touching any part of the symbol, draw a smooth line that curves from left to right.

8. This is the hood and back of the dragon; when finished, it is almost a half circle. This half circle is the full length of the front part of the symbol.

9. Back at the top of the page, you are now going to draw the dragon humps.

10. Starting one and a half inches from the beginning of the outer line, draw a half circle and then another half circle. The two are joined where they touch the long line. They resemble two humps (9, 10).

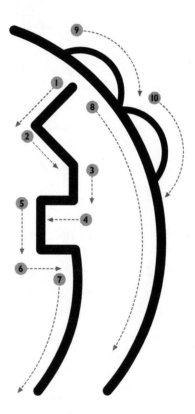

Sei-He-Kei

Symbol 3: Hon-Sha-Ze-Sho-Nen

Hon-Sha-Ze-Sho-Nen appears in the shape of a tall building and resembles the human body. When literally translated it means, "No past, no present, no future." This is fitting, as Hon-Sha-Ze-Sho-Nen is used to transmit energy through space and time. In order to do this it must always work in the spiritual plane, where there is no concept of past, present, or future. By using this symbol, past-life traumas can be reprogrammed to effect a healing in the present, thereby literally changing our future. You can direct the healing to repeat as often and for as long as you desire by stating that you "desire this healing to be repeated every half hour for twenty-four hours" (or any other time span).

When working in the spiritual plane, center yourself, which is just another way of saying get into a comfortable position. Close your eyes, take a deep breath, and let your thoughts wander where they will. Visualize or draw the Hon-Sha-Ze-Sho-Nen in your mind, and state your request. If you want to go back to a certain period or time, that's what you ask for. For example, when my carotid artery was blocked, I requested to "go back in time to the period right before that clot was formed." Stating your destination tells your consciousness where to stop. It is a subtle feeling, but you know when you have reached the particular time period. While in that time I acknowledged that I had a perfectly healthy body, enjoyed good health, and my blood circulated freely through my body. I visualized the Hon-Sha-Ze-Sho-Nen symbol again and asked to be brought back to the present time, with my body in this complete, healthy state.

The universe does not recognize the words *no* or *not*. So, in stating your request, you must always state it in the positive. If you phrase it with a negative you will create the opposite. If, for instance, I had stated, "My body does not have a blood clot," the universe would have dropped the not and interpreted it as; "My body has a blood clot." Always phrase your desires in a positive manner. Sometimes this takes some creative thinking.

The combination of opening the third eye and working in the spiritual plane with the Hon-Sha-Ze-Sho-Nen often brings about spiritual or psychic experiences. A student of mine frequently sees the spirits residing in his house. He talks to them and often directs them to leave a room, which they do. He said that one evening while he was relaxing and just drawing the Hon-Sha-Ze-Sho-Nen for practice, he suddenly became aware that he was watching a gorgeous woman getting into her shower. When he became fully aware of what he was doing, he swiftly and uncomfortably was brought back to his body. He called me and told me what happened. I explained that by visualizing the symbol while in this relaxed state, he had an out-of-body experience. When he became aware of what he was doing, he became frightened and quickly returned to his body. He asked me if he could ever do it again. I assured him that once a person has these experiences, they usually recur. He became excited and wanted to know just how he could get back to the girl because he didn't get her phone number!

As you can see, this symbol is a little more complicated than the other two, but if you learn it in parts, it becomes comparatively easy. I break it into three parts—the top, middle and bottom—which seems to work with the students I teach in person.

Part I: I will number these lines as I describe them, because at times you have to go back and cross a certain line.

1. Top to bottom, draw a straight two-inch line (1).

2. Right to left, draw a straight three-inch line (2).

3. In the left lower quadrant, draw a one-inch line that angles at forty-five degrees from right to left and up to down (3).

4. Repeat a mirror image of the same line in the right lower quadrant of the box that the first two lines have formed (4).

5. Cross the bottom of line 1 with a straight line a half-inch long from left to right (5).

6. Directly below the symbol, draw a straight three-inch line from left to right (6).

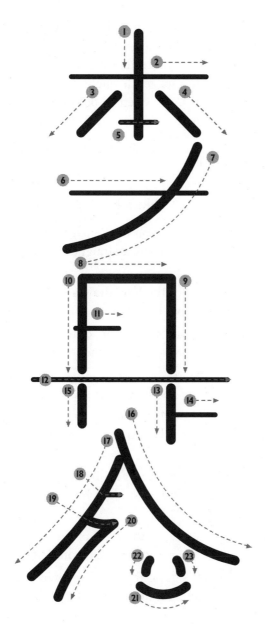

Hon-Sha-Ze-Sho-Nen

7. This next line crosses the right side of line 6. It starts a half-inch above the line on the right side of line 6, angles gently downward to cross line 6 about two inches, continues its gentle angle for about another half-inch then swings to the left to be completed where line 6 started, but half-inch below (7).

This completes part one of the symbol. Practice this part a few times and then continue.

Part 2: This segment looks like a house on a foundation.

1. Using the middle section of the page, directly below line 7, from left to right draw a straight line two and a half inches long (8).

2. At the right side of the line, draw a straight line from top to bottom three inches long (9).

3. Back at the left side of the line, draw a straight line from top to bottom, two and a half inches long (10).

4. Halfway up line 10 on the right side of the line, from left to right draw a straight half-inch line (11).

5. Just slightly below this "house," from left to right and starting an inch to the left of line 10, draw a straight line (12).

6. On the right side of the line, directly under but not touching line 9, draw a straight line, one-inch long from top to bottom (13).

7. Halfway up line 13, to the right of the line, draw a straight line a quarter of an inch from left to right (14).

8. Back to the left side of the symbol, directly below but not touching line 12, draw a quarter-inch line from top to bottom (15).

This completes part two of the symbol. If you number your lines as you draw them, it will avoid confusion. Practice and then continue.

Part 3: This segment looks like a tent with a smiley face on the inside.

1. For the last section, directly in the middle of the page, from top to bottom, with a gentle curve from left to right draw the right side of the tent. This is from three to four inches long (16).

2. Starting on the left side and a half-inch from the tip of line 16, from top to bottom, draw a line that gently curves from right to left, completing the tent (17).

3. On the left inside of the tent, three quarters of an inch from the top, draw a quarter-inch line from left to right (18).

4. This next line resembles a large 7, only you gently curve the top of the 7 and gently curve the long part of the 7. Again, on the left side of the tent, a half-inch below line 18, attaching the tip of the 7 to the wall of the tent, bring the tip of the curved 7 in from left to right one quarter-inch (19).

5. Then going from top to bottom, gently curve the long part of the 7 from right to left, following the line of the tent, or line 12 (20).

6. On the inside of the tent, on the lower right side, draw a half-inch line from right to left that curves like the smile on a happy face (21).

7. Above and on the left side of line 21, draw a line quarter of an inch long, from top to bottom, curving slightly in from right to left (22).

8. Above and on the right side of line 21, draw a line one quarter-inch long, from top to bottom, curving slightly in from left to right (23). Lines 22 and 23 should be the "eyes" on the happy face, and the curves should be facing each other.

This completes the Hon-Sha-Ze-Sho-Nen. It is the most complex symbol of Reiki II, and it works in the most complex field.

It is well worth your time and trouble to master this unique symbol.

Reiki healing session

Both hands, with the palms down, are always used in a healing session. Fingers and thumbs are extended and held together, as if they had socks over them. They are placed in the Reiki hand positions and rest there gently, completely relaxed, with no exerted pressure. Remember, unless you have a license to touch (medical, massage, minister), the hand positions are used about an inch above the client, with no touching. Should you feel a need to rest your hands directly on the client, you must ask for permission to do so. Once the hands are in position, turn on your intent "Reiki on" to heal, and the energy will start to flow. The energy continues to flow as long as your intent is there. When the session is over, remove or withdraw your intent.

With your hands in a Reiki position, you may feel a multitude of sensations, which could include heat, cold, tingling, color, sound, or any other physical sensation. This is just your response to the energy flowing through you. Some practitioners feel nothing at all, while the person receiving the treatment feels the sensations. We're all different.

While your hands are in position, mentally draw a picture of each symbol, while saying the symbol's name. I sometimes use my nose, or draw them with my eyes, while my hands are maintaining the position. The sensations last for three minutes or so. As a rule of thumb, I usually keep my hands in one position while I mentally draw each symbol three times. If the flow continues past three minutes, it means you have reached a place requiring a lot of healing, and you are not going to accomplish this in one session. Continue on with the sessions, and when you are finished inform the client that there is an area that is going to require more treatments. People do not get sick in a day, and often they are not going to be cured in a day.

My favorite story concerns a woman who began attending our Reiki exchange evenings. When she walked into the first session, she could barely move. She had an oxygen tank running continuously and walked like a crippled old lady. It took several of us to get her onto a table for treatment. She had been diagnosed with a multitude of lung problems and had just fallen and broken a rib. After the first session her pain had decreased to the level where she no longer required pain medication. When she returned for her second session, she could move better, but she was still dependent on her oxygen. After her second session she went to her doctor and he x-rayed her. Much to his amazement, her rib had completely healed in just over two weeks. When she arrived for her third session, we did not recognize her. Although she carried her oxygen with her, she did not use it once during the evening. Better yet, she could walk upright with no pain, her hair was done, and she had even applied makeup.

We always have a Reiki story segment as part of our evening, where people can tell their Reiki stories or share anything they choose. This woman told us exactly what happened during and after her Reiki treatments and ended by saying, "When I first came here, I was looking for a miracle. Now I know I have found one." By the way, this woman went on to become a Reiki practitioner to continue her self-healing and to share healing with others. Always honor your intuition during a healing session, and if your hands want to go someplace that is not a recognized hand position or want to linger, do what you feel is proper. Remember, Source is guiding the session, and often Source tells us what to do.

Some Reiki masters teach you to hold each hand position for five minutes. Right now, stop reading and set a timer for five minutes. Don't do anything until the timer rings. Five minutes is a long time, especially when your are holding your hands an inch or so above someone's body. My rule of thumb is to hold the hand position while you mentally draw each symbol three times. This way the session does not exhaust either you or the client.

When you have finished with the front positions, ask the client to turn over, and do the back positions. Only if I feel the need, or if the client has complained of hip, knee, ankle, or foot problems do I Reiki the lower extremities. The exception is the bottom of the feet. By reversing the Cho-Ku-Rei and putting your hands on the soles of the client's feet, you can draw out negative energy from the client. This is an excellent way to complete a healing session.

Do not be surprised if the client falls asleep, starts snoring, or cries or moves around during the session. This is all part of the Reiki energy working.

When you are finished with all the positions, bring both hands back above the head. Turn your hands sideways and in a gentle manner sweep your hands down, across the body. When you

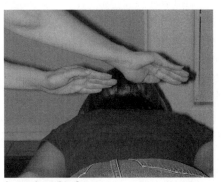

Sweeping the Aura

get to the feet, move your hands off to the side and shake them vigorously. This is called cleaning or sweeping the aura. You shake your hands to get rid of any negative energy from the client's aura.

Gently have the client sit up and keep him or her sitting until stable. Oftentimes a person feels a little woozy after a healing session. Always offer the client water and encourage him or her to drink as much as possible after the healing session. The body releases toxins during the healing session, and the water helps eliminate the toxins from the body. As a matter of fact, it's a good idea if you drink water, too.

After the session I usually tell the client what I noticed. I do not diagnose, but I will say things like, "You really pulled a lot of energy when I was over your abdomen. Are you having any stomach problems?" Or, "Your back really pulled a lot of energy, does your back hurt?" In this way I share what I found without scaring the client. Let the client talk to you. If they have problems, let them share them with you. Emotional issues often surface during a session, and sometimes the client needs someone to listen. Of course all of these conversations must be held in the strictest confidence.

Sometimes during a healing session the practitioner will feel the energy arc back to his or her body. Do not be alarmed. Just grab the energy in your hand, turn away from the client, and shake the energy off of your hands. You can always dispose of energy by shaking it from your hands.

Distance healing and more

With the Reiki II initiation, contact with other realities begins. The healer learns to access the universal consciousness of this world and other worlds for information and help in healing. The Reiki II healer moves beyond the limits of his or her body. If Reiki I changed your life. Reiki II changes who the healer is in relation to the world. Everyone is stretched by Reiki II, and everyone grows.

Everything in the universe is composed of energy. When you receive your attunements, it's like plugging directly into the universal current. You can do this simply by having the intent to use or access the energy. The Source within you is in direct contact with the universal Source, which has no limits. This is how you can access your timeline, perform healing sessions, and give and receive attunements. There are no barriers to what this energy can do. We are the ones who put barriers on the energy by our thoughts. I compare this to a light switch. When you turn on the switch, the light turns on, when you turn it off, the light goes off. Just because the switch is off doesn't mean there is no electricity there. It is not being used, but it is always ready at the flick of a switch. So it is with the Reiki energy. If you can think it, try it!

The major teaching of Reiki II is healing. Simply put, it means you act as the generator to send Reiki healing anywhere in the universe, simply by your intention to do so. There are many ways to do this, some very complicated, some very simple. My favorite is to create a rose. Being on the Internet and belonging to many healing groups, I receive healing requests every day. As I receive each request, I print it out for my convenience. When I have a pile of requests, I sit down, relax, put my hands on the pile, and close my eyes. I then mentally ask each of the recipients if they will accept a Reiki healing, adding that if someone does not desire the healing it will go to someone who wants and needs it. I then visualize a rosebud and mentally draw the Hon-Sha-Ze-Sho-Nen superimposed over the rose bud. This opens the path the healing energy will take to get to the recipients. I state my request that this healing energy be delivered to each of the names on the list and request it to repeat every half hour for twenty-four hours. I close by mentally drawing the Hon-Sha-Ze-Sho-Nen again, while I watch the rose slowly open. When the rose is fully open, I thank Source by saying, "And so it is." I open my eyes knowing everyone on the list has received a healing session.

At the close of our Reiki exchange nights, everyone sits in a circle as I guide the group through a long-distance healing session. I have everyone close his or her eyes and picture a rose bud. I ask the practitioners there to visualize the Hon-Sha-Ze-Sho-Nen symbol. Anyone who has a healing request now says the names out loud. I wait until everybody has stated his or her healing requests. Then I request this energy be directed to those who are willing to accept it, and if they are not, that it goes to someone who wants and needs it. I ask Reiki to repeat the session every half hour for twenty-four hours. I ask all practitioners to visualize the Hon-Sha-Ze-Sho-Nen. Next, I ask everyone to see the rosebud opening, knowing when it is fully open the healing sessions will be sent. Again, I thank Source and have everyone open his or her eyes. The energy level in the room is phenomenal.

You can use pictures, names, lists, oral requests, or anything else to send the energy. All you really need is a sender (you), a willing receiver (anyone) and a link to Source (Reiki).

I start my day with a self-healing Reiki session. Right before I start my session, I ask for this energy to heal me and anyone else I designate. I never waste any Reiki energy if I can send it to someone else. Sometimes I designate this energy to be used to heal our world. I feel each one of us makes a difference in helping to restore order to this world.

Every human on earth is a part of, and connected to, every other human. To illustrate this, picture a huge string of Christmas tree lights. The electrical cord is our connection to each other, and the lights are our own individuality. Some of us are red, white, yellow, green, blue, purple, and so on. We each shine with our own special light, connected to each other by the cord. The sad part is that when one of our lights is removed, the whole string shuts down, *and so it is with us!* When one of us is ill, we all are, so it is vitally important that we reach out and heal ourselves and each other.

Our universe is dependent on each and every one of us. As we heal each other and ourselves, we slowly heal our world. If we think of healing the whole world, it seems like an insurmountable task. But if we think of healing just one person a day, it becomes a task we can handle. With thousands of us healing one person a day, the world will soon be healed.

Manifesting

The universe is yours to command. It always stands ready and willing to give you anything you want, anytime you want, anywhere you want. What holds you back? You do. How? By believing your conscious mind when it tells you that you do not deserve anything you desire. When you believe abundance is a reward instead of a fact of life, you spend your life judging all your actions. With this mentality, every time you fail you are punishing yourself for some real or imagined "bad" action, thereby justifying your failure. When you perceive yourself as a failure, you also make a mental quantum leap and label yourself as undeserving. The thought goes something like this, "If I can't even do this right, I don't deserve to be rewarded." Sound familiar?

By believing in a limited universe, you believe there is limited amount of abundance available. You view life through the "pie" mentality. By believing that all of abundance is one big pie, and there are only so many pieces available, you spend your life in a futile effort to get your piece of the pie. Abundance means "being in great supply," and you live in an abundant universe. There is more than enough for every person on this earth if you can get past your own preconceived notions of good and bad, limited and limitless, and deserving and undeserving.

When you find yourself guilty, you punish yourself much worse than any judge or jury would. Oftentimes the punishment is a life spent in quiet despair, without any hope of parole. Forgiving yourself and moving on is the first step in learning to live without judging yourself.

If, in your heart of hearts, you do not believe you deserve something, then there is no power on earth that can obtain it for you. You must always honor yourself and believe in your own worth. If not, even if you achieve your desire, it tarnishes and you lose it.

There are three questions you should answer before you try to manifest anything:

1. Is this what I really want?

2. Is this something I think I should have?

3. Do I feel I deserve this?

If the answer to any of those questions is no, do not try to manifest at this time, because you will only sabotage yourself. The ability to manifest does not ever come from a feeling of need or want. It comes from the quiet place within yourself that knows you are the creator, actor, director, and audience of your life. That little place that says, "I know," which you so often ignore, is your center of creation.

Remember, you manifest with your thoughts. When you have a thought and express it as a desire, you put the wheels in motion for its appearance in your life. The thought goes out into the universe, and the universe starts the preparation for the manifestation. The universe does not work on a time schedule. Manifesting is not always instant gratification. The universe gives us what we desire in any manner it chooses.

A recessed chin is a maxofacial deformity, which is prevalent in my family. Growing up, it was my most intense desire to have what I considered a normal chin. When I was in my mid-forties I started experiencing terrible neck, arm, and hand pain. My arms would go numb and turn blue, and my neck and head would hurt so badly, that I often hit my head on a wall to feel the pain outside my head rather than inside. After making the round of doctors, neurologists, and neurosurgeons, I was told I had fibromyalgia, and I would just have to live with it.

Finally a friend of mine suggested I see her dentist. I did, and he diagnosed me as having TMJ. He made a stent to realign my bite, and my pain disappeared. I was ecstatic and asked if there was anyway I could have my mouth fixed permanently. My dentist referred me to a maxofacial surgeon who operated on me and realigned my bite by surgically bringing my chin forward. My mouth was wired shut for eight weeks, and then I went through two years of orthodontics. I went through a terrific amount of time, pain, and money to finally get what I had asked for many years ago. I now have my new chin. Do I really like it? No. Why? Because it changed the way I look. Even though I didn't like my old chin, I was used to the way I looked and was more comfortable with myself. The old adage is true; be careful of what you ask for because you just might get it.

There are studies to prove that if you land a jet plane in the jungle where people have no conception of what a jet plane is, they just won't see it. It's not that they ignore it, they simply don't see it. A jet plane is not in their reality; it is not something they can imagine. Therefore, to them, it is not there. Our brains work the same way. If we cannot imagine it, we cannot experience it. So when you are manifesting, make sure you ask for something in your reality.

If you want a brand new car but somewhere deep inside you feel you don't deserve a new car, you will never manifest one. Manifesting is like planting a garden. When you state your desire, you have planted the seeds in your garden. When you begin to doubt your ability to create what you desire, you run out to your garden and dig up the seeds you have planted. No wonder your garden doesn't grow!

You need to work on your self-worth before you work on the new car, because no matter what you "put out there," it will be destroyed by your feelings of worthlessness. You are the only one who holds yourself back, and you are the only one who can stop doing it.

If you are at the point where you find you are constantly sabotaging yourself and would like to stop, now is the time to do so. Find a quiet place, sit down, relax, close your eyes, take some deep breaths, and ask yourself why you feel so unworthy. Usually some situation will come to mind. When that happens, acknowledge the fact that this situation is part of your life experience and part of you. Do not reject it or label it as anything other than part of yourself. Say to yourself: "This _____ is a part of me. I love and accept this part of me. I acknowledge I need this to feel whole." Feel the experience integrate within you, feel the release, and know you have assimilated a part of you that has been sabotaging you for a long time. Most of us have many experiences that contribute to our feelings of worthlessness. In order for this to work, you must suspend your judgment and condemnation of the incident. Truly forgive yourself.

Continue bringing to mind other instances where you have judged yourself harshly, acknowledge that this is a part of you, and you accept and love this part of yourself. There is no good or bad, only experiences, and you must own and acknowledge all your experiences as components of who you are. Only then can you release the feelings of being unworthy, undeserving, or bad. Only then can you learn to love yourself.

Once you have cleared your emotions, you will find you really are deserving of that brand new car and can now take steps to manifest it in your life. The key part of the phrase here is "can now take steps to manifest it in your life." The universe always grants our desires, but we must take the steps to have our desire manifested in our three-dimensional world.

If it is your burning desire to win the lotto, then in order for the universe to fulfill your desire, you must purchase the ticket! A student of mine explained it this way. The universe will provide all the food you can eat, but you are the one who must bring it into your house and cook it.

Desiring the perfect mate is only the first step in finding one. Once you have decided what qualities you want in a partner, you must then leave your house and mingle with others, so you and your perfect mate can find each other. He or she certainly will not come charging into your living room riding a white horse! The universe is willing and able to grant all of our desires, but we must do our part in manifesting those desires in our three-dimensional world.

I want to say something about affirmations and visualizations and the way they work. If you want a new car, sit and visualize it. Smell the upholstery, see the key in your hand, fill in all of the details, and decide this is what you really want. What's stopping you from getting it? You've heard that athletes use visualization to achieve superior results. Magic Johnson visualizes the basketball going through the hoop before he ever throws the ball. It usually does. What is the difference between his visualization and your visualization? He is visualizing something he has already accomplished and knows he can do—while your are visualizing a desire and are not really sure if you can manifest it. It is much easier to visualize and manifest something once you have been successful doing it.

Affirmations work in the same way. I am sure you have been told that if you tell yourself something long enough, you will believe it and create it. This is called reprogramming your computer brain. The problem with this is your brain may be reprogrammed, but your emotions are not. We do not create with our brains, we create with our thoughts—two different things. No matter how many times you tell yourself you weigh 120 pounds, (if you weigh 150 pounds), when you look in the mirror you still see all 150 pounds of yourself, and all the affirmations go out the window. When I first started to use affirmations, I had a tape that explained if you repeated an affirmation to yourself three hundred times, your mind would be reprogrammed, and you would create what you desire. I would actually sit and count off the times I said the affirmation. I never got what I wanted. Why? One, I was so busy counting I was not focusing on what I was desiring, and two, I didn't really believe what I was affirming. Remember, it has to be in your reality.

Use the Sei-He-Kei symbol when you want to clear your emotions before manifesting. It is the emotional symbol and is a wonderful tool to balance your emotional self before you start. Once your emotions are balanced and you decide what you want to manifest, visualize the Hon-Sha-Ze-Sho-Nen symbol to get in touch with your innermost self. It is from this place of quiet and knowledge that you create. State exactly what it is you want. Do not ask, do not plead, and do not beg. Simply state your desires, with the sure knowledge that this is now in the process of being created.

We can never create from a negative. Feelings of desperation, need, and panic are considered negative feelings. We create or manifest because we *know* we can. Remember, you are Source, and there is no one or nothing in this universe or all other universes combined that can deny Source. Once you have this concept, go for it! When you express your desire, know it is already created, and you are just waiting for the manifestation in our three-dimensional reality. Source does not operate on our time. Just relax and know that what you have created you will receive.

Before we leave manifesting and healing, I want to make a statement. *Fear, not released, must manifest as experience!* So often we hold back our words or thoughts because we "don't want to put anything bad out there." This is wrong, because what we usually hold back is something fear-based. An example is, "I'm going to fail at my new business, job, marriage, etc." We are taught not to think about failing for fear of creating the situation. If you try to repress your thoughts, you are denying the pink elephant in the living room. By not letting yourself think these fearful thoughts, you are repressing them, holding them to you, and giving them added power. By telling yourself not to think about something, you automatically ensure it is the only thing you will be thinking about. If you hold that thought or energy to you, you *must* then create what you fear.

You must follow your thoughts through and envision your fear, *without acting on it*. When you have pictured, recognized, and assimilated the fear, you have released the need to create it in this dimension. Do not dwell on it, just release it. Let's say that you are afraid of failing in your job. If you relax and close your eyes and see yourself actually failing and, perhaps, getting fired, it releases the emotion the same as if you had actually failed in real life. It's like watching a film of yourself experiencing your fears. The release is the same. If you do not understand this, read the above over and over until you do. This is so very important to how we live and what we create in our lives. Just because you have thought of something, especially something with a strong emotion attached to it, doesn't mean it has to be manifested in your life. If you fear it, just release it and accept the fear as part of yourself. We have a dual nature, and in order to be healthy, we must be in balance. Being in balance means recognizing and accepting both aspects of ourselves. By doing this we never bury our fears, we only accept them.

Remember, I said we consciously create from our place of quiet and knowledge, and we unconsciously create from our emotions, especially strong emotions like fear. The key here is to try to balance the peace and serenity we obtain with our conscious mind with the fears and turmoil of our unconscious mind. We are the only ones who can balance our emotions and we can only do that by recognizing and admitting that *all* emotions are a part of us. Allow yourself to be you, allow yourself to be.

Beaming

Beaming is the process of standing apart or away from a person or object and directing the Reiki energy straight to them. To do so, hold your hands together, palms outward and thumbs touching, turn on the Reiki energy with your intention to deliver Reiki, and direct your hands where you want the energy to go. This is very effective in accidents, when you cannot get near the injured party, for clearing the energy in a room or in the hospital where the client may be hooked up to a lot of equipment, or anywhere else you would like to send energy without being in direct contact.

I beam when I am called to deliver Reiki to a patient in the hospital. Usually, the person is hooked up to IVs, monitors, tubes, and a lot of bulky medical equipment. It is impossible to get close enough to do a hands-on healing session. I have stood to one side, started beaming, and have instantly seen changes recorded on the heart monitor. Since it can get uncomfortable for the practitioner to stand in one position for any length of time, I suggest you change your position in the room while you are beaming. You can usually go from one side of the room to the other or to the foot of the bed to change positions.

If you pass by an accident on the road, you can put your hands up and immediately beam healing energy to those involved in the accident and those who are trying to help the injured parties. A single hand will do, if you're driving. Often on the highways you might see an injured animal along the roadside. It is not always possible to stop for the animal, but you can beam healing energy to it.

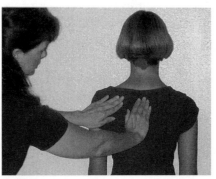

Beaming

I like to beam Reiki to the planet. Whenever I'm walking or just sitting outside relaxing, I put my hands in the beaming position and send healing energy to mother earth and the whole planet.

Reiki II Attunement

When you feel ready for your attunement, sit in a quiet room on a straight-backed chair, with your arms and hands comfortably in front of you. If you have the Reiki video, put the cassette in now. Take a deep breath, turn on the video, and relax. You will feel subtle changes in the energy around you. It is often beneficial before the attunement process to have read the attunement steps, so you will be familiar with what is happening during the video. This will remove any fears you may have about the attunement process.

1. I stand in front of you, channeling the energy and directing it to your whole body.

2. I walk around your left side and put my right hand on your right shoulder.

3. I work above your crown.

4. I put my hands on your crown.

5. I put my hands on the back of your head.

6. I put my hands on both of your shoulders.

7. I put my hands directly over your heart.

8. I walk around to your right side and put one hand on your forehead and one hand on the back of your head.

9. I walk to the front of you and hold your right hand, palm up, in my left hand.

10. I work over your hand and slap the palm.

11. I repeat this three times.

12. I put your right hand down and pick up your left hand in my left hand.

13. I work over your hand and slap the palm.

14. I repeat this three times.

15. I put your hands together, palm to palm, envelope them with my hands, completely encircling your hands.

16. I blow down the fingertips of your hands.

17. I point your hands up and hold your fingertips with my hand.

18. I readjust and hold your fingertips with my hand.

19. I angle your fingertips and point to your heart, forehead, and crown. You will feel my breath in all three of these places.

20. I walk to your back and ground you.

21. I walk around to your front, and you will feel a motion in the energy.

22. When all is quiet, open your eyes.

When you open your eyes, put your hands in front of you, one on top (palm down) and one on the bottom (palm up). Separate them between six to twelve inches. Now, say to yourself, "It is my intent to use Reiki." You will feel the energy flowing between your hands. If someone were to put his or her hand between your hands, the energy would be felt flowing from your palms and you would feel the block of energy from the presence of that person's hands. Play with this energy. Form an energy ball, see if you can find its limits, but most of all, enjoy it.

Remember, the attunement process has again altered your energy pattern. You may experience some of the detoxification symptoms mentioned in Reiki I. Drink plenty of water, pamper yourself, and perform Reiki on yourself. The symptoms will disappear as your energy pattern stabilizes.

Congratulations. You are now a Reiki II practitioner.

SUMMARY

Reiki II introduces the first three Reiki symbols: Cho-Ku-Rei works primarily in the physical plane. Sei-He-Kei works primarily in the emotional plane. Hon-Sha-Ze-Sho-Nen works primarily in the mental or spiritual plane.

Using these symbols opens the door to long-distance healing and timeline travel. Each of these symbols are slapped into your palm during your attunement, thereby sealing Reiki into you for life.

You no longer have to be physically present to heal or to send energy to anyone. You can mentally form the intention to send Reiki anywhere in the world, and the energy must follow your intention.

Reiki allows you to manifest your desires in this three-dimensional plane. You can now rid yourself of the unwanted baggage of old, repressed fears, and emotions. With the release and integration of these old fears, you are free to create whatever you desire. Reiki has taught you how to travel back in time to correct mistakes and forward in time to deposit energy. This energy awaits your arrival at the specified time in the future.

Beaming allows you to send Reiki to a specific place without touching the object of the energy. This is especially useful in hospitals or when you are driving and pass an emergency on the road.

Your second-degree attunement completes the pathway for the energy to flow out of your palms. It also stimulates the pineal gland to awaken your spirituality. This awakening assists you in sending energy with your thoughts. In other words, you are now certain you and Source are one, and there is no duality in your life.

Once you have received your attunement, you can now earn your living performing Reiki healing sessions. Remember, there always must be a fair exchange for services.

Congratulations on becoming a Reiki II practitioner.

CHAPTER SEVEN

Reiki III: The Masters Course

When you work
you are a flute
through whose heart
the whispering of the hours turns to music.
... And what is it to work with love?
It is to weave the cloth and threads
drawn from your heart,
even as your beloved
were to wear that cloth.

—Kahil Gibran, *The Prophet*

Welcome. I honor your decision to become a Reiki master, and I thank you for choosing me as your master and teacher. It is an honor and one I value highly. By choosing me as your master, we have created an unbreakable bond and I will always be there for you. This is not a guru/disciple relationship; it is, however, a lasting relationship formed by two equals, who support each other's endeavors. Once you have obtained the master level, you assume a larger responsibility for your life's actions. In order to teach Reiki, you must live it; in order to live it, you must have absolute trust in Reiki's energy.

You are now starting on your voyage to become a Reiki master. You will soon receive the master attunement and be given the master symbols. The master-level attunement not only boosts the level of energy, it also expands your vibrational field to include communication with other universes. You will experience some major energy shifts with this attunement.

But this class is much more than just an attunement. You will learn to live the precepts of Reiki at a time when the peace obtained by the healing Reiki power is so sorely needed. It will be your responsibility to pass this peace on to the rest of the world.

There are four essential qualities of a master healer: trust, faith, love, and humility. As a Reiki master you are now the pathway of the healing energy called Source. In order to effectively function as the guardian of such tremendous energy, you must have absolute trust in the Reiki healing power as well as the faith that you are capable of working with and teaching others how to do likewise. Although different healers may channel the energy by a variety of different methods, none can teach or heal without love and humility. You must learn to love the hardest person in the world to love—yourself. There is no ego in using or teaching Reiki. You are the co-creator of the healing process, allowing the Source within to join the Source without, and exit through you, thereby balancing all it comes in contact with.

By becoming a Reiki master you have made a commitment to be of service to others. You will be living the five precepts of Reiki, for you must live it to teach it.

> Just for today, I will not anger.
> Just for today, I will not worry.
> Just for today, I will give thanks for my many blessings.
> Just for today, I will do my work honestly.
> Just for today, I will love all living things.

As a Reiki master and trainer I have added one more principle:

> Just for today, and the rest of my life,
> I will strive to be an example,
> of love, kindness and caring, to all of humanity,
> so that all will know, by observing my life,
> that I am a Reiki master.

This is the heart of the commitment I expect from all of my master-level students. This does not mean you have to live like a monk. We are here to experience all facets of life to the fullest extent and enjoy every minute of it. As a master, I expect you to add decorum to your experiences. Many Reiki masters teach that Reiki is a spiritual, blessed, holy, or serious business, and I certainly do not dispute their teachings. Reiki is part of who and what we are. Good health is a serious business, but it is only one aspect of our being and should always be separated from our religious beliefs.

Because Reiki deals not only with the physical body but also the mental, emotional, and spiritual bodies, I consider Reiki spiritual. This means we are dealing with more than we can see, taste, or feel. One of the reasons Reiki is not accepted by the medical community is because Reiki is often intermingled with the spiritual beliefs of the master. *Reiki is a healing modality using the Source energy within and of the universe to re-establish the balance of energy in the dis-eased person, place, or thing.* Your own spiritual beliefs should be separate from your Reiki teachings unless you are intentionally combining them. If you are purposely slanting your teaching to integrate your spiritual belief system, you must make this fact known to you students. An example would be Christian Reiki. By announcing your belief system in the title of your class, you are informing everyone who applies that your class is heavily flavored with Christian concepts.

This course teaches what I refer to as bare-bones or pure Reiki. Some of my students who have become masters have added crystal healing, aromatheraphy, or their own dogmas to their Reiki practice. This is fine, as long as you advertise your Reiki courses as such. Some of my masters only want to appeal to a certain segment of society, and they tailor their courses to coincide with the belief systems of this segment. This does not present a problem and does not dilute Reiki, as long as you are honest from the beginning about the theories you are adding.

There is one other thing I would like to address, and that is the competition for students that is beginning to appear in the Reiki community. Many masters appear to be in a rush to entice students to enroll in their classes any way they can. You can often hear them denigrating another master. I do not think it is wise or appropriate to judge or criticize others who are doing their best to advance the healing practice of Reiki. All masters who are teaching Reiki, living Reiki, and promoting the principles of healing and understanding on this planet deserve our honor and recognition. When the student is ready, the appropriate master for them will be found.

Wherever you are in your Reiki instruction, I honor what you have learned, as I honor all Reiki practitioners. All I ask is for you to think about everything I teach you, run it through your heart, consider how it feels to you, and either accept it or reject it honestly. As each of us has a different signature, face, and body, each of us will find the right way to practice Reiki.

No matter what symptom the illness expresses, Reiki always treats the cause and not the symptom. There is no dis-ease too serious or too severe for Reiki to treat. My oldest sister and I were discussing Reiki and she wanted to know if I had any successes curing people. As I was telling her about some of my clients, I noticed she was having difficulty swallowing. I asked her if she had a sore throat. She said yes, she did. I performed a Reiki healing session on her, and soon she was swallowing without pain. I said, "See, Reiki works." She said she could see how Reiki could cure a sore throat, but not how it could cure a person with heart disease! It makes no difference what you label the symptom, Reiki can and has cured it. *If* Reiki can cure a sore throat, then Reiki has to be able to cure heart disease. If it works for one, then it must work for all. You cannot be selective and state that Reiki can only cure minor ailments. If one is cured, then all must be cured.

The cause of all illness is a disturbance in the energy flow of the affected organ. Reiki re-establishes the normal, balanced flow to that organ. An example of this is anger. When a person gets angry, the blood vessels constrict, the heart rate speeds up, the veins and arteries become engorged, and adrenaline begins to pump through the system. Anger is handled in two ways: we either explode and vocalize our anger, or we bury it deep down in ourselves. If we explode, the anger is released, and our body returns to its normal state, with minimal damage to our physical body. Of course, we may not be very popular with the rest of the human race! Most of us do the socially acceptable thing and bury our anger internally.

This is the beginning of the dis-ease process. We do a slow burn, which is exactly what happens to our body. Our vascular system is affected, since the constriction and engorgement of the blood vessels is prolonged. Our heart rate is still high, and the adrenaline that was released but could not circulate, due to the constriction of the blood vessels, is still floating around in our system. We are literally burning our body and are certainly out of balance. The internal organs, so dependent on our blood supply for oxygen for cell regeneration and to carry away the toxic end products of cell growth and reproduction, are suddenly deprived of the fresh, clean flow of oxygenated blood. Their life-giving processes are slowed down or even stopped, resulting in dis-ease in the affected parts of the body. We can get away with this a few times because of our body's natural recuperative ability, but who gets angry only a few times in their life? Like putting bricks together to build a wall, we abuse our body repeatedly each time we get angry and do nothing with the energy except bury it. We do not know how to handle or discharge our anger and end up with a dis-ease process.

Reiki, by re-establishing the energy balance of the body, tears down the bricks, releases the pent-up energy, and balances the affected area, allowing the body to heal itself as it was intended to do. As with anger, a similar process occurs with any extreme negative emotion we experience.

When you teach and practice Reiki you are actually defusing the emotions before they can cause bodily harm. As humans we will always experience a vast array of emotions, but with Reiki we can give our bodies one more option on how to handle these emotions. By living Reiki you will learn to feel the emotion, recognize it for what it is, and let it flow through you with no adverse effects. This is the reason the emphasis is on living Reiki as you teach it.

As a master, it is better to offer to teach people Reiki than to perform repeated healing sessions on them. It's like the old saying, "Give a man a fish and you feed him for today; teach a man to fish and you feed him the rest of his life." If someone requires repeated healing sessions, it is more convenient for them to be able to give themselves a session anytime they require one. By teaching them Reiki I, and instructing them in self-healing, you are giving them the option to participate in their own wellness.

As a Reiki master there are two basic precepts that must be part of your curriculum:

1. The person must ask to be treated. Because Reiki works on so many levels simultaneously, we must always have permission to work with and enter a person's energy fields. This is not the same as the person believing in what we are doing, it only means we cannot invade someone's energy field without his or her permission. Everyone has the right to choose what will happen to his or her own body.

2. There must be an exchange of energy for services—never for healing. The healing is done by Source in combination with our physical body and we provide the service to the client. The exchange can be money or an exchange of services or objects. Simply stated, an exchange of energy is taking place. Reiki practitioners who offer healing services on a professional level establish a fee. The fee sets a value on the service, which ultimately reflects the feeling of worthiness of the person seeking to change his or her state of health. What you establish as your fee is strictly up to you. You must do what feels comfortable for you. A lot of Reiki practitioners have an intense desire to help change the universe and therefore feel awkward charging a fee. Remember, you can help others and still charge a fee. If you put no value on your services, neither will anyone else!

All of you, as Reiki II practitioners, are familiar with the basic principles of Reiki and should be comfortable performing Reiki healing sessions. One of the major differences in the Reiki III level is the ability to work in the different bodies and energy fields. There are four that bodies we always treat in Reiki. They are the physical, spiritual, mental, and emotional. These four bodies are contained within the human body and psyche. The seven spiritual bodies you will be learning about are bodies outside the human body.

The *physical body* is the one we are most familiar with and therefore think is the easiest to treat. Wrong. Our physical body is our three-dimensional reality. It is the part of us we can see, feel, and experience. Our symptoms and dis-eases appear in and on our bodies and are very, very real to us. When we are in pain, we know it and want the pain stopped! We are taught to go to the doctor or take a pill for relief, and we want the relief to be instantaneous. We forget that the pain pill does not get rid of the pain, it only stops the brain from recognizing the pain. Whatever part of you hurts continues to hurt, you just don't recognize it. The pill or shot blocks the neural pathway of the pain to the brain. This causes the brain to not recognize the pain. The pain is still there but temporarily not felt by the body. Pain pills or shots are always temporary. After a period of time this blocked neural pathway is opened, and the brain again recognizes the pain.

As a society, we take massive amounts of antibiotics, which suppress our immune systems and set up the condition for more disastrous infections. Antibiotics do not kill the entire invading organism, just deter them enough to make us feel better. The organisms left are smart and want to survive, so they mutate. Then we're dealing with a more potent organism, which needs a stronger antibiotic, which still doesn't kill all of the invading organisms, and so on. All this happens while compromising our immune system! Or better yet, let's just cut out the dis-eased organ and expect our body to function as if it were complete! These are quick cures; I just don't know how effective they are over the long run.

Reiki works by balancing the energy in physical body, and the results are not always immediate. There are many different reasons why we develop the dis-ease processes that we do, and these reasons are often unconscious and complicated. Most of these dis-ease processes have taken a long time to develop and will take time to dissipate. Reiki is not a quick fix but a permanent healing modality. When we are back in balance, we are cured.

Reiki is holistic, meaning treating the whole person, to effect a cure. Often in performing Reiki healing sessions, I have been told it takes too long to get the desired result! I reply that dis-ease takes a long time to manifest.

The most difficult part of working with the body is dealing with and accepting the belief system of the client. Everyone concerned must understand that Reiki is a healing modality that works by restoring balance to our bodies, minds, and spirits. There are no magic pills or mutilating surgeries, just the knowledge that we have the ability to heal ourselves and effectively assist in the healing of others.

The *spiritual body* is the body we must first work through. Only then can we begin to treat the cause of dis-ease and not its symptom. Reiki affects the main cause of dis-ease by working through what psychology chooses to call the psyche, or the human mind as spirit. Psychologists also label the psyche as anima, soul, subconscious, inner self, or pneuma. We know there is a link between our thoughts and our physical well-being. People who are prone to pessimism, anxiety, sadness, anger, and stress are more prone to develop dis-ease. A poor state of mind is often the cause of physical dis-ease. People who know they are going to get ill or catch something always do. Why? Because the body must do what the mind demands.

Our human body is our higher consciousness or spirit manifested in a physical form. For the higher energies to be able to flow to an individual, there has to be a connection to Source or higher consciousness. When Reiki works on this higher consciousness (spiritual body), it calms the nervous system and opens the system to be able to integrate the higher energies, which are essential for the flow of Reiki energy. It is virtually impossible to heal an individual who stops or shuts off this flow of energy by refusing to be treated.

When we access the *mental body,* we start to balance the emotions, bringing peace, clarity, serenity, and dissolving confusion, fears, and depression. Behavior patterns, both new and old, are often brought to light through a series of Reiki sessions. We begin to examine these patterns, accepting and rejecting them as we desire. We learn to live in the now, for yesterday is gone and tomorrow may never come. The Five Principles of Reiki begin to make sense—Just for Today. We let go of the chaos created by our old, toxic behavior and experience a sense of well-being and self-esteem. When we focus on the present, we focus on the now, who we are, how we feel, and how our body reacts.

An emotion is a thought linked to a feeling or sensation. A sensation usually occurs in the present; but with the help of our human memory, we can remember and project old emotions to the situation. An example would be: I am sick (present experience). I was sick like this before and ended up in the hospital (past experience). Will I die (future experience)? Usually, if we are experiencing serious dis-ease, the thought of death crosses our mind. When we think of our own deaths we often experience an intense fear. By working on the emotional level, Reiki can nullify that fear. This allows us to accept our present dis-ease on a more rational level. When we are rational about our dis-ease process, we can start to cure it. Fear inhibits a cure.

Many people experience a huge amount of anger when they are told they have a life-threatening illness. How often have you heard that many people's first reaction to being told they have AIDS or cancer is denial, and their second reaction is anger? This is true. We get angry because we do not want to die, and we can't understand why we are the ones who contracted this killing disease. Why me? How many people blame someone or something else for their illness? How many use their illness for their own benefit? How many really want to get well? As long as a person is in the state of anger or denial, she or he can never be cured. Why? Because these intense emotional states cut off and block the flow of energy. The healing energy is denied admission to the body and therefore cannot re-establish the body's sense of balance.

Part of what we do as Reiki masters is teach our clients and students to live in the now while dealing with and releasing old emotional wounds. When we teach someone to choose, on a mental level, how to react to old hurts and pains, we teach how to release this emotional, painful grip. When we mentally choose to release old emotions, we begin to choose health instead of disease. The brain picks up the conscious desire for change and is now choosing to be well. This conscious choice allows for growth, healing on a cellular level, love of life and harmony.

> I love myself. I am right and perfect. I forgive myself for past errors. I am loved and lovable. I am good. I am caring. All who come in contact with me realize who I am, that I am love embodied in a physical form.

How do the above statements sound to you? Do you agree with them? Can you say them, out loud, in all honesty, about yourself? Or are you mentally thinking, "Yeah, right!"

What we feel about ourselves is reflected back at us by what people think of us. If we cannot state, in all honesty, that we love ourselves (warts and all), then we need to redefine ourselves to heal our emotional body. Only then can the focus of the pain shift to love, acceptance, and health. Love, on the emotional and physical level creates a vibration harmonizing with the pituitary and pineal glands that enhance healing on all levels. First, each one of us must sort through our emotional baggage; then we must help our clients and students to do so also.

One way to learn to love yourself is to fall in love with yourself. The bathroom usually has a large mirror and a shelf. When you know you will not be interrupted, go into the bathroom and close the door. Light a candle or two, then turn off the light. Look at yourself in the mirror. Look deeply into your own eyes as you would the eyes of your lover. As you are looking into your eyes, say out loud, "I love you." If this feels funny or you don't believe what you are saying, keep trying. I know someone who did this everyday for a month before she became comfortable saying that she loved herself. If you do this long enough, one day you will feel yourself falling in love with yourself. This is a tremendous growth step.

As you can see, the spiritual, mental, and emotional levels all seem to deal with our thoughts and emotions. There is a very fine line separating these levels. Combined they form our subconscious, conscious, and supraconscious minds.

Our subconscious mind is the part of our personality consisting of complex feelings and desires. We are usually unaware of what is stored in our subconscious mind, thereby making these complex feelings and desires unavailable to our conscious mind. Our conscious mind is oriented to person, place, and time and is acutely aware of our external surroundings. Supraconsciousness is our spiritual aspect.

Any of these three levels of consciousness can and do give directions to the body. The body then responds to these directions by creating illness or health. The body does not care which level of consciousness gives the order. Because many of these orders for illness come from the subconscious mind, we are often sick without knowing or realizing that our thoughts created the illness.

For this reason, I stress the importance of working on the emotional level while performing a healing session on the physical body. All dis-ease has its origin in our emotions. This is where we, as masters, go to cure.

Sit in a quiet place, close your eyes, and take a deep breath. Stay still for a while. Gently open your eyes and read the following meditation.

I never confuse what I seem to be with who I really am. I am never the poor, struggling human, which is what I seem to be. I am host to the indwelling power of Source. I still the movements of my body, slow my breathing, and softly fall into the very core of my being—my center of consciousness. In this place of infinite calm I join with Source and view my world. Although thoughts are appearing in a never-ending stream, I allow them to pass by my field of vision. I know that I do not create these thoughts. They come to me from the Universal Mind and are directed to my consciousness.

I know I attract each thought that passes by. I know I may choose any thought I desire. I only have to decide, and the thoughts and images I have chosen are directed to me. If I choose to accept any idea, it will manifest in my world. I, and I alone, choose what I will think. By choosing what I think, I thereby create my world. I know I can refuse any thought I choose, thereby barring the door to any negative thought passing by. I have complete confidence in my ability to choose my thoughts, thereby creating my reality. I do not predict when or where my thoughts will materialize, I only know they will. My every thought and decision is answered from a perfect and inexhaustible Source. I know I am the earthly vessel for this magnificent power; therefore, I know I create everything that happens in my life. I am Source having a human experience, and for this I am truly grateful.

Seven spiritual bodies

A Reiki master also works with and heals within the seven spiritual bodies. These bodies surround the physical body and influence what is permitted to enter and leave the physical body.

This energy field is usually collectively referred to as the aura or etheric body. The aura is a luminous body that surrounds and interpenetrates the physical body and emits its own characteristic radiation.

Each layer of the aura is associated with a chakra. A chakra is a vortex of energy dispersed throughout the body to charge and direct the energy that enters it. There are seven major and twenty-one minor chakras dispersed throughout the body. We will be dealing with the seven major chakras, which are located in the spinal cord. They are the root, sacral, solar plexus, heart, throat, forehead, and crown.

Every other layer of our energy field, or aura, is highly structured, like standing waves of light patterns, while the layers in between appear to be composed of colored fluids in constant motion. Thus, the first, third, and fifth layers all have a definite structure, while the second, fourth, and sixth are composed of fluid-like substances with no particular structure. They take on form by virtue of the fact that they flow through the structure at odd layers and somewhat take on the form of the structured layers. The seventh layer is the exception. This causal layer is composed of a gauze-like substance that connects us to all of the other bodies in the universe. It cannot be measured or contained. Each succeeding layer completely interpenetrates all layers under it, including the physical body. Thus, the emotional body extends beyond the etheric body and includes both the etheric and physical bodies. Our emotions not only affect our physical body, but penetrate through our etheric body as well, affecting the very core of our being.

Each layer of the spiritual body can be considered a level of higher vibrations, occupying the same space as the level below it and extending beyond. This simply means that the physical body and the etheric body are interconnected. You cannot peel one layer off as you do an onion, it is impossible.

Since our thoughts create our reality, anything entering the body must first travel through these seven levels. In other words, whatever we create is created out of the infinite potential of the universe. When we send our desire to this infinite potential, it manifests what we have asked for and sends it to us through our spiritual bodies.

The seven bodies are:

1. **Ka:** a complex field of energy whose primary form is similar to the physical body, only larger. Called the etheric or spiritual twin, the Ka is an energy field that is an exact duplicate of the human body. One theory says that the Ka is formed and grows before the human body; in other words, our body is created in the likeness of our Ka. This field is located about an inch above the physical body and is the one you will be working with the most.

2. **Pranic Body:** a field that extends a few inches to several feet from the physical body. This is what is usually seen in auric photographs. The size of the pranic body is determined by the emotional state of the body and changes accordingly. Since the size of this body is determined by our emotional states, it is often difficult to

work in this body and to determine where the emotional body begins. There is a legend that Buddha had an aura of over three miles. Can you imagine working in that pranic body?

3. **Emotional Body:** a field that is slightly larger than the pranic body. The line of separation is not clearly defined. The emotional body is a storehouse for our emotions. It can become clogged if our emotions do not flow easily through this body. This is the body we clear when we clear our emotions. Have you ever released an emotion and actually had a physical reaction to that release? The release comes through the emotional body. This is the reason that clearing the emotions is so important in healing the body. If we do not clear the emotions out of the emotional body, they have to manifest in the physical plane.

4. **Mental Body:** a field that is slightly larger still, because it holds memory holographically in space around the physical body. This is the body we tap when we do past-life regressions, have flashbacks of old memories, or peek into the future. Since all of our lives are being lived simultaneously, this body allows us to access past or future lifetimes as well as past or future events in this lifetime.

5. **Astral Body:** a subtle sheath that is just barely larger than the mental body. As the name implies, this is the energy that leaves the body when we project or travel.

6. **Etheric Body:** a field that works in the etheric plane. Ether is an all-pervading, infinitely elastic, massless medium, formerly postulated to be the medium of propagation of electromagnetic waves. This is the energy used to manifest our creations. When there is a time lag between our thought to create and the manifestation, it is because our creation is being formed in this body and does not instantly appear in our three-dimensional reality.

7. **Causal Body:** the least dense of the bodies. This body is infinite and connects us to all the other bodies in the universes.

Scanning

As healers, we work with these bodies, because virulent or long-term illnesses are often "caught" while manifesting in these outer bodies. To prevent the body from becoming dis-eased, we remove these orbs of energy before they reach the body. It is an easy matter to just grab these energy balls and pull them out of the aura.

With the client lying on his or her back, put your left hand on his or her right shoulder. Visualize the Reiki symbols. You are now co-mingling your energy with your client's energy. This co-mingling of energies gives you permission to work in his or her energy field. Position your right hand, palm down, about an inch above the body. Start at the head, and slowly move your hand down the middle of the body. The direction is always from head to foot.

It is amazing what you feel when you do this. Sometimes it feels like a tingle, and sometimes it feels like you are hitting a brick wall, the mass in the energy field is so strong. You will be able to feel any "knots" of energy. When you do, wrap your hand around the knot, pull your hand out of the energy field, and vigorously shake the energy from your hand. The client will feel this release. Pick, pull, and shake. You may have to go down the same path several times before you clear the middle of the body. Once you have cleared this part, start on either side and continue to scan and remove this energy. Some Reiki masters teach you to scan the seven layers. I do not, because the energy passes through all layers before entering the body. If you scan the first two layers, you will catch whatever is on its way to the body before it enters.

I suggest that you work in these subtle bodies when there is an emotional aspect to the dis-ease process you are treating. When your client is fragile and you don't want any other dis-ease process entering his or her physical bodies, thereby compounding the illness, or when you are treating a dis-ease process that just doesn't seem to get better no matter what you do, working in the spiritual body is very beneficial. Do so anytime you feel the need to!

One fun thing to do is have your client lie flat on his or her back. Standing on the right side, place your right hand on his or her shoulder and your left hand on the hip. Mentally bounce the energy from your right to your left hand. I like to move my head and look at each hand as I am bouncing this energy. You can feel the energy bounce, and so can your client.

Scanning

Often when I am finishing a Reiki treatment, I will ask another practitioner to sit at the client's feet while I sit at the client's head. I put my hands on the crown and have the other practitioner put his or her hands on the feet. I "run" the energy through the body, while the other practitioner is "pulling" it from the feet. This is quite an experience.

The Master Symbols

In traditional Reiki, you are given one master symbol; I give you two—the traditional master symbol, plus the symbol I use to ground my attunements. Traditional Reiki does not teach grounding of the attunements.

When I was first attuned, my Reiki master did not ground me. For days after my attunement I was wide open to all the energy around me. I could actually hear conversations in other cars while I was driving. I often felt someone else's emotions, particularly fears. I had no way to close and protect my crown. My crown finally closed naturally, but I will never forget how scared and uncomfortable I was.

In my practice I have discovered that if you do not ground the attunement, the student is left wide open and often becomes very spacey. This state sometimes lasts for as long as they practice Reiki. I have two students who were attuned by other masters and not grounded. They did not practice Reiki at all, because they felt so woozy when they used any of the Reiki energy. I attuned and grounded both of them, and they now practice Reiki without any problems. I want to thank Diane Stein for sharing the grounding symbol with us and for the groundbreaking work she has done for Reiki.

Dai-Ko-Myo

The master symbol Dai-Ko-Myo (*day-ko-mayo*) is used for all healing and spiritual work. Once you have mastered this symbol, it can replace all the other symbols. Often this is the only symbol used in healings, although the Hon-Sha-Ze-Sho-Nen can still be used for sending energy. This master symbol encompasses all other symbols and is said to have the power to stabilize energy on all levels simultaneously. It heals dis-ease from its highest level, or first cause. Both the traditional and non-traditional versions of the symbol are presented here. I request you use them both and decide for yourself which one you are more comfortable with.

The traditional version was taught by Mrs. Takata. I have seen several versions of this symbol, and they all resemble each other. I will teach you the one I was taught. This version resembles a house or the body in an upright position. As you are drawing it, you will be able to feel the downward progression of the energy.

I found the newer version in Diane Stein's book, *Essential Reiki*. I tried it, and it felt more comfortable to me. This is the predominant symbol I use. As you draw the spiral, you will be able to feel the energy spiraling out from the center and dispersing into the universe.

Each of the symbols targets one of the vibrational levels:

1. Cho-Ku-Rei resonates to the physical level. It is the opener.

2. Sei-He-Kei stirs the emotional body. It is the straightener.

3. Hon-Sha-Ze-Sho-Nen works with the mental and spiritual body. It transcends distances.

4. Dai-Ko-Myo works on the spiritual level or first cause, which is where we create all that we are. Since this symbol works on the spiritual level, it is very important in the attunement process, because we are actually opening the student to Source.

5. Raku is used for grounding.

Raku

I was taught the Raku (raa-coo) was to be used only for attunements, and then, only for grounding purposes. I have since discovered otherwise. This is the grounding symbol used at the end of the attunement to ground your energy. For this reason alone, it is a very valuable symbol. It came to my attention that when we are working in the spiritual plane, we often feel a little unfocused afterwards. The Raku is an excellent symbol to stabilize energy anytime we are operating in the spiritual sphere. If you are performing a healing session and there has been a lot of emotional release, draw the Raku over the body after you have swept the aura. This grounds all of the emotions that have been released, and appears to stabilize the client's energy.

If you do any out of body work and do not "fit" in your body when you return, use this symbol to pull yourself all the way back into your body.

This symbol is called the Raku and resembles a lightening bolt. Lightning (electrical energy) always goes to ground. This symbol takes our energy and sends it to ground.

Drawing the Reiki Symbols

Symbol 2: Traditional Dai-Ko-Myo

Since this is a complicated symbol, I will explain it in three parts and label all the lines for convenience. Look at the drawing of the symbol while you are reading the directions.

Part I:

1. Two inches from the top of the page, in the center, draw a straight line, three inches long, from left to right (1).

2. Lines (2) and (3) meet and form a triangle one inch above the line. Cross the line and extend the triangle another inch and a half from the bottom of the line. Line (2), the left side of the triangle flows downward from left to right. Line (3), the right side of the triangle, flows downward from right to left.

3. Lines (4), (5), and (6) are all enclosed within the large base of the triangle. Each line is an inch long and starts a half-inch below line (1). Line (4) is a straight line on the left side of the triangle. Line (5) is the middle line and has a slight right-to-left curve. Line (6) is on the right side of the triangle and has a more pronounced right-to-left curve.

Part II:

1. Line (7) is a straight line, from left to right, three inches long, in the middle of the page.

2. Line (8) is an inch-long straight line, top to bottom, underneath but not touching line (7), slightly left past the middle of line (7).

3. Line (9) is an inch long, curved from left to right, top to bottom, under but not touching line (7), slightly past the middle of line (7).

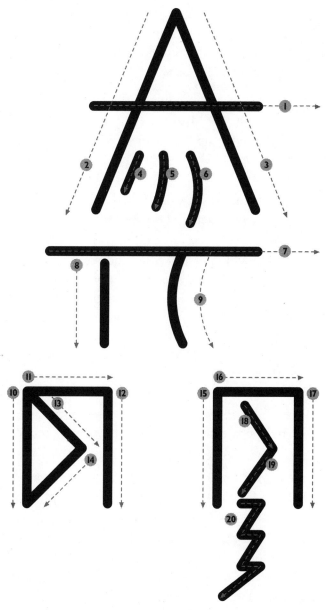

Traditional Dai-Ko-Myo

Part III:

This part looks like two boxes sitting next to each other. Each box has three sides, and no bottom. I will refer to these boxes as the left and right boxes.

1. Line (10) is on the left side of the left box, running top to bottom for two inches.

2. Line (11) is the top line of the box, and connects to lines (10) and (12). It is one inch long and runs from left to right.

3. Line (12) is the right side of the left box, runs top to bottom for two inches and is connected to line (11) at the top.

4. Lines (13) and (14) are within the box and form half of a diamond. Line (13) starts a quarter inch from the top of the left side of the box and is angled left to right and down, forming the top of the diamond. It stops a quarter-inch before joining line (12). Line (14) starts at the right end of line (13) and angles back to the box, from right to left and downward, where it attaches to line (10), thereby completing the half-diamond shape on the inside of the box.

5. The right box is almost exactly the same as the left box.

6. Line (15) is the left line of the right box.

7. Line (16) is the top line of the box and connects lines (15) and (17).

8. Line (17) is the right side of the right side box, runs top to bottom for two inches and is connected to line (16) at the top.

9. Lines (18) and (19) are within the box and form a half-diamond. Line (18) starts a quarter-inch from the top of the left side of the box and is angled right to left and down, forming the top of the diamond. It stops a quarter-inch before joining line (17). Line (19) starts at the right end of line (18) and angles back to the box, from

right to left and downward and stops slightly left of mid-line (this is the only difference in the boxes so far), completing the half-diamond shape on the inside of the box.

10. Line (20) starts at the bottom end of line (19) and zig-zags in a downward motion for six lines. It looks like a lightning bolt with a long tail.

Symbol 3: Non-traditional Dai-Ko-Myo

This is a spiral with a telescope on the top.

1. Line (1) starts in the middle of the page as a small circular spiral and completes after two and a half circles. The spiral ends with the circular line on top.

2. Line (2) attaches to line (l) where the upward sweep of the last spiral starts to turn from left to right. Line (2) comes up, from bottom to top, for an inch, then sharply angles to the right, stopping about an inch above the end of line (1).

Non-traditional Dai-Ko-Myo

3. Line (3) travels from top to bottom at the edge between lines (1) and (2). Line (3) is no more than three quarters of an inch long (to fit in this opening), and the top of the line has a slight curve from right to left, ending in a point. The bottom half of line (3) starts at the point then angles downward with a slight curve from left to right.

4. Line (4) is a lightning bolt, one inch long, drawn from right to left, and is situated in the hump formed by lines (1) and (2). This means it is to the left of line (3), in the middle of the space created by lines (1) and (2).

Raku

This symbol has only one line. Line (1) starts at the top of the page and travels from top to bottom. It is a large lightening bolt, with two very distinct bends in the bolt. When using this symbol, I usually draw it from as high as I can reach to the floor, behind the student. The power of this symbol lies in the fact that it puts the practitioner directly between heaven and earth. Picture the practitioner standing with one hand extended to the sky and the other pointing to the earth. In reality, this is what each healer is and does. We take the power from above, run it through our body to unite with the power in our body and give it back to the earth. How powerful, how beautiful, how wondrous and how true.

Every healer stands alone, combining and directing the all powerful healing energy. Yet, every healer is directly linked to every other healer in the universe. The Raku makes us aware of the awesome energy we direct, each time we perform a Reiki healing session or attunement. This is very humbling!

The Dai-Ko-Myo is used for healing. It is also the symbol that combines and replaces all other Reiki symbols. The Raku is used in the attunement process and whenever you want to ground yourself or a client. Both traditional and non-traditional symbols are presented here to give you a choice.

The traditional symbol has all the beauty and majesty of a Japanese work of art. The non-traditional symbol is more modern and has a wonderful feel when you are drawing it. They are both very powerful symbols, and I ask that you try them both and choose when and where to use each symbol. Do not take the easy way out and only learn the simpler, non-traditional Dai-Ko-Myo or you will deprive yourself of the grace and beauty of the traditional symbol.

Once you achieve master status, the Dai-Ko-Myo can be the only symbol you use. Often it is the only symbol required in a healing, although I like to use the Hon-Sha-Ze-Sho-Nen for long-distance healing. The Dai-Ko-Myo can be used to transmit healing power long-distance, but I love the lines and grace of the Hon-Sha-Ze-Sho-Nen. The choice is always up to you.

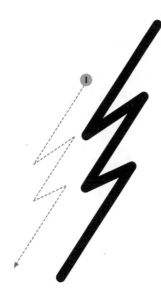

Raku

SUMMARY

1. Cho-Ko-Rei resonates strongest to the physical body.

2. Sei-Hi-Kei resonates strongest to the emotional body.

3. Hon-Sha-Ze-Sho-Nen resonates strongest to the mental or spiritual body.

4. Dai-Ko-Myo resonates with First Cause or the Source within.

5. Raku is used to ground energy.

The seven spiritual body levels contain the blueprint or template from which the physical body is derived. Healing at this level makes for profound changes, the type commonly labeled as miracles.

The Raku is becoming popular with American Reiki masters. It is shaped like a lightning bolt and acts like one, by taking energy and going to ground. It is the arc between heaven and earth. Using this symbol to ground a new student acknowledges that this new Reiki practitioner stands between the two worlds. "As above, so below" is now personified in the new practitioner. Each of us is a "bolt" of magnificent power with the knowledge and capabilities of joining heaven and earth to facilitate a healing. As the bolt passes through the body it cleanses, strengthens, heals, and regenerates the body. What a wonderful gift to give, and what a wonderful way to end an attunement.

CHAPTER EIGHT

Teaching Reiki

My name, and my place,
and my tomb,
all forgotten,
The brief race of time well
and patiently run.
So let me pass away, peacefully, silently,
Only remembered
by what I have done.

—Bonar, *Leaves of Gold*

In order to become an effective teacher you must intimately know your subject matter. The simplest way to do that is to read books on the subject, practice Reiki, and get in touch with your guides for direction and guidance with your teaching. It is also very beneficial to talk to and work with other Reiki practitioners. Sharing energy and stories increases our knowledge while binding us together.

Reading other books about Reiki puts you in touch with all the different ways available of presenting similar material. Read and run it through your heart. If any concept does not feel good to you, do not adopt it. If it makes sense and feels good, then you might want to incorporate it into your teachings.

Practicing Reiki gives you valuable experiences. You learn first hand what this fabulous energy can accomplish. With practice comes confidence. I never knew of a Reiki master who did not spend at least a year practicing before teaching.

Everyone is surrounded by guides. Some people refer to these guides as angels. Upon receiving your master attunement, your Reiki guides attach themselves to you. If you spend any time in meditation, you will feel their presence and influence in your life.

Their presence is subtle; they do not knock you over your head, yet they can become the most powerful influence in your life.

To get in touch with your guides, get into a comfortable position and relax. Concentrate on your breathing and go deeply within your consciousness. State that you would like your Reiki guides to come forward and make themselves known to you. Continue meditating. When you feel the meditation is over, open your eyes.

Your guides may contact you while you are meditating or anytime they choose. All of a sudden you will just know they are there. Remember to meditate without expectations. When we think we know how we are going to be contacted and it doesn't work out that way, we think we have failed. Just be open to any way your guides may choose to contact you.

Each one of you will be teaching the same subject slightly differently, because we are all different, and our thoughts, personalities, and belief systems will affect our teaching style. I suggest you begin by making a course outline for each level you are going to teach. Include all the information you want to cover in each course. Be very specific with this. If you choose to add a belief system to your Reiki teachings, be sure to include this in your presentation.

As long as you adhere to the basic principles of Reiki and use the attunement system to create new practitioners, you can define the contents of your course any way you choose. You have the option of adding concepts to your class course at your discretion.

One of my masters incorporated the Christian concepts into her Reiki training courses. She calls her course "Reiki for Christians" and is very successful. By titling her course "Reiki for Christians," she is advertising the fact that this particular Reiki study incorporates the Christian ideology and anyone who does not subscribe to this ideology need not take her course. Another master teaches "Animal Reiki." There are classes in Crystal Reiki, Hands-on Reiki, Massage Reiki, and many others. The only rule is to be up front with what you are teaching. You could have some very disappointed students if you are teaching Christian Reiki and the student is a Buddhist.

Once you have an outline and know the direction of your teaching, write out your course content. It is best to break up your courses into Reiki I, Reiki II, and Reiki III. Make a booklet for each class to be given to the students. The students really appreciate having everything you teach in writing so they can take it home and read it any time they choose. Remember that you are teaching a lot of material in a short period of time, and everyone doesn't learn at the same pace. The biggest complaint I have heard about other Reiki masters is that they do not hand out any preprinted material and students feel they cannot listen, learn, and write at the same time.

I begin my classes by telling my students to put away their pencils and papers and that everything I will be teaching is included in the course booklet they are receiving. This ensures that they are relaxed and paying attention to what I am saying, not trying to capture my words on paper. You can incorporate the cost of printing the booklets in the price of your course. Students have repeatedly told me they would much rather pay a few extra dollars for the booklet than not have one available. Until you create your own teaching materials you can use this book as an outline or guide.

Now that you know what you are going to teach, you have to find a place to teach it. There are New Age learning centers scattered across the country and these are good places to start. If there is one in your area, contact them, and present your credentials and course outline to see if they would like to sponsor you as one of their facilitators. Another good place to look is at any New Age bookstore. Many of these bookstores sponsor classes to subsidize their book sales and are always looking for new facilitators. These learning centers and bookstores usually either charge you a fee, or take a percentage of your class tuition, or both. The centers and bookstores provide the space, advertise the classes, and are available to answer the phones to enroll the students in your class. In turn, you provide flyers, help with the advertising, and teach the class. It is usually a convenient, profitable way to do business.

If there are no learning centers or bookstores available, you can always start teaching classes in your home. You are now responsible for your own advertising, providing the space for the classes, and being available to answer the phone to enroll the students. Of course, an answering machine can record your calls while you are out. By teaching from your home, you are in control of when you want to schedule your classes, and you keep all of the class tuition.

Printing flyers and posting them in supermarkets, libraries, and any store that will allow you to is a good way of advertising your class schedule. Mailing out flyers is more expensive, but you reach a larger number of people by doing so. In my home area it costs four cents a flyer to hire someone to hand-deliver your flyers to homes. This is practical in large housing developments.

There are many ways of advertising your class schedule. Radio is a moderately expensive way of reaching a large number of people. Buying ads in the movie theaters is another effective way of advertising. For those with a big budget, there is always television.

One way of attracting students is sponsoring a Reiki exchange night. I have held these in my home, my office, my personal growth center, and the centers where I facilitate classes. These nights are free to all participants. All practitioners are invited, along with any person who is interested in Reiki and wants to know more about it before taking a class. The evening starts with a small history of Reiki and a summary of what Reiki is. The practitioners then perform a healing session on the newcomers. These evenings offer two valuable services to the community. First, Reiki practitioners now have a place to come and practice their Reiki, and second new people receive a free healing session and get to experience first hand the wonderful power of Reiki. It really is a win-win situation. If you possibly can, I encourage you to consider starting a Reiki exchange night in your community.

Passing Attunements

Attunements should be performed in a quiet room, free from distractions. Some masters attune several people at one time, and this is perfectly acceptable. If I am physically passing the attunement, I like to attune each student separately. As I am fond of saying, do whatever feels good to you. There is no right or wrong way, just the way your heart leads you. Before I pass an attunement, I like to clear the room. I do this by drawing a large Cho-Ku-Rei on each wall. I usually put a straight-backed chair in the middle of the room, as I will be walking around the chair. I Cho-Ku-Rei the chair to clear it of any negative energy. If I have time, I like to burn some sage in the room. It leaves a pleasant odor and releases negative energy. If I do not have the time, I clear the negative energy with a series of Sei-He-Kei's. All of these will work equally well.

I escort the student to the chair and explain a little of what I am going to do. I tell the student she or he will feel me moving around, that I will be holding his or her hands, and that when I am finished, I will say to open his or her eyes. I take a few minutes here to allay any fears the student may be experiencing. We often talk about what is going to happen and how it will affect the student. Since a lot of people travel during the attunement process, I

The Heart Position

tell them to take their time opening their eyes. I now tell them to close their eyes, take a deep breath to center themselves, and relax and enjoy the process.

The heart position is the basic attunement position. In this position your right hand, with the fingers and thumb together, is pointed upward and positioned slightly to the right of your heart on the right side of the breastbone. This hand is actually touching your body. Your left hand is extended upward and outward, with the hand at a right angle to the wrist. You then move the left hand until you connect with the external Source energy. You will feel when the connection is established. Unless you are actively using your left hand, it stays in this position, drawing the energy from the Universe to and through you, throughout the attunement.

In traditional Reiki I there are four separate attunements. I will teach you all four, then I will teach you the combined one I use. The choice is always up to you. Instead of writing out the full names of the symbols, I will use the first letter to represent the whole symbol.

1. S=Sei-He-Kei
2. C=Cho-Ko-Rei
3. H=Hon-Sha-Ze-Sho-Nen
4. D=Dai-Ko-Myo
5. R=Raku

When passing the attunement, mentally draw the symbols as you are saying the full name. Remember to keep your eyes open. I have observed Reiki masters close their eyes while mentally drawing the symbols and, in the process, start swaying, lose their hand positions, and almost fall on the seated student.

First Attunement, First Degree, Traditional

After establishing the heart position, while standing in front of the student, with your right hand, draw a large C, ending with the palm of your hand beaming at the student's heart. At this point I ask my Reiki guides to help attune this student.

1. With hands in heart position, walk around the student's back or left side.

2. Put your right hand on the student's right shoulder, project the D, H, C, S, to adjust your energy and the student's.

3. Place your right hand over the student's crest (at the crown) and mentally project the H symbol, followed by the S symbol.

4. Mentally project D, H, C, S, slightly above the student's head, without moving your hand from the crown position, two to five times or until you feel the heat.

5. Gently come off the student's head, position your hands in the heart position, back off two steps, and walk around the right to the front of the student, being careful not to touch him or her. Resume heart position.

6. Straddle the student's feet.

7. Lift both of the student's hands by placing the fingers of your right hand around his or her wrists.

8. Holding the student's right wrist with your left hand, move your fingertips to his or her fingertips, wrapping the thumb out of the way. The student's fingertips should be tucked into the first joint of your fingertips.

9. While holding the student's fingertips, mentally project D, H, S, C.

10. Move your right hand over the student's fingertips until the fingertips are in the center part of your palm, grasping the fingertips firmly. Repeat D, H, S, C.

11. Slide your right hand back to the student's right wrist.

12. Holding both of the student's hands by the wrists, angle the fingertips to the forehead (don't allow the fingertips to touch the forehead).

13. While inhaling, form the C symbol by drawing it with your tongue.

14. You are going to divide the exhale into three short breaths.

15. Blow part of the breath over the student's fingertips to the third eye.

16. Blow the second part of the breath between the student's arms to the heart, moving his or her hands to allow you to do this.

17. Lastly, point the student's fingertips at the hairline and blow the remaining breath to his or her crown area.

18. Hold the student's hands together gently for a few seconds, then lower to the lap.

19. Say, "When you are ready, you may open your eyes."

(Note: Traditional Reiki does not use the grounding symbol.)

Second Attunement, First Degree, Traditional

1. Repeat steps 1 through 3.

2. Bring your left hand down and place the middle of your palms on the ridge of the student's shoulders on both sides of his or her head. Repeat H and S.

3. Repeat D, C, H, S three to four times.

4. Mentally project symbol D over the student's head and then run C, H, S down into his or her heart.

5. Repeat D, C, H, S three or four times. You are opening the student's heart and can't repeat this sequence too many times.

6. You might feel the energy moving; do not be surprised.

7. Assume heart position and come around to the front.

8. Repeat steps seven through nineteen.

(Note: Traditional Reiki does not use grounding symbol.)

Third Attunement, First Degree, Traditional

Explain to the student that this attunement is similar to the first two, but that this time when you go behind him or her, you will press lightly against the back of his or her head. Ask the student to please continue to keep his or her head erect.

1. Repeat steps one through three of the first attunement.

2. Bring your left hand down.

3. Form a triangle with the thumbs touching at the bottom of the triangle and the first two fingers forming the sides of a triangle touching at the fingertips. Place the triangle form at the back of the student's head, encircling the bony part of the skull (occipital). Your thumbs should be resting right below the ridge of the skull.

4. Mentally project H and S.

5. Repeat the D, C, H, S sequence two to three times (no more than three times). Heat may be felt.

6. If the back of head is in alignment with your own third eye, immediately move out of alignment, and do not look through the triangle with your third eye, as this is the back door to the student's third eye.

7. This attunement is very expanding and may be disorienting.

8. Gently remove hands.

9. Repeat steps seven through nineteen of the first attunement.

The first and second attunements may be done together. The third and fourth are always done separately.

Fourth Attunement, First Degree, Traditional

1. Repeat numbers one through three of the first attunement.

2. Walk around student until you get to his or her right side.

3. Place your right hand over the student's forehead with your palm over his or her third eye and your left hand on the back of his or her head, above the occipital ridge.

4. Project the H and S symbols.

5. Repeat several D, C, H, and C symbols.

6. Remove the hands gently.

7. Draw the C symbol over the student's head.

8. Assume the heart position and go around to the front of the student.

9. Repeat steps seven through nineteen from the first attunement.

(Note: Traditional Reiki does not ground the attunements.)

First Attunement, Non-traditional

This attunement is a combination of all four of the first degree attunements. The combination is a very effective way of passing the Reiki I attunement. Explain to the student that he or she will feel you in front, in back, and to the sides, that you will often be touching him or her, and that when you are finished you will ask for the student to open his or her eyes.

Your hands are in the heart position unless you are actually using them for the attunement process. Your right hand is at heart level, a little to the right of your sternum, with the thumb resting against your body and the fingers pointing up and together. The left arm is extended straight up, with the hand at a right angle to the wrist. The left hand is moved like an antenna until you connect to the universal energy and feel the flow coming through your left hand.

1. In the heart position, attune to the energy and feel it coming into your left hand.

2. Facing the student, with your right hand, draw a large C, ending with the palm of your hand directly over his or her heart.

3. Ask the Reiki guides to attune this student.

4. Walk around the left of the student to the back.

5. Place your right hand on the student's right shoulder. Your left arm is still in the air.

6. Use D, C, H, S to stabilize your energy with the student's.

7. With your right hand, draw a large C over the student's crown.

8. Gently rest your right hand on the student's crown, lower your left hand, and rest both hands on his or her crown.

9. Repeat the D, C, H, S symbols three to four times each. Lift both hands up an inch or so, to ensure you feel the heat emanating from the newly opened crown.

10. Gently remove your hands from the crown.

11. Form a triangle with your thumbs touching and your fingertips touching.

12. Place this triangle on the back of the student's head with your thumbs resting right below the ridge of the skull (occipital ridge).

13. Repeat D, C, H, S three to four times.

14. Gently remove hands.

15. Place one hand on each shoulder and repeat D, C, H, S three to four times.

16. Rest a hand on each shoulder and gently slide the hands down over the heart, until your fingertips are touching.

17. Repeat D, C, H, S three to four times. You are opening the heart and can repeat the sequence as often as you feel necessary. Often you will feel a huge change in the energy as the heart opens. Sometimes it feels as if the energy is moving your hands. This position allows you to brace the student in case he or she should fall forward while the heart is being opened. Lift both hands about an inch from the newly opened heart to ensure that you feel the energy.

18. Gently remove your hands and assume the heart position.

19. Walk around the student to the right side.

20. Gently place your right hand over the student's third eye and your left hand over his or her occipital ridge.

21. D, C, H, S three to four times. This opens the third eye. There are times you will actually feel this eye opening. Opening this third eye allows the student to start using his or her psychic power.

22. Gently remove your hands, assume the heart position and walk around to the front of the student. Always walk to the right of the student.

23. Pick up the student's hands, which should be together as if praying, with your left hand, and place the fingertips in the first digit of your right fingertips. Hold the student's hands with your right hand, and put your left hand back into the air.

24. Mentally project D, C, H, S three to four times.

25. Move your right hand over the student's fingertips until his or her fingertips are in the palm of your right hand. Again, put your left hand in the air while holding the fingertips with your right hand.

26. Mentally project D, C, H, S three to four times.

27. Holding the student's hands by the wrists, with both your hands, angle his or her fingertips to the forehead. Do not allow the fingertips to touch the forehead.

28. While inhaling, form the C symbol by drawing it with your tongue inside your mouth. You are going to divide the exhale into three segments.

29. Blow part of the breath over their fingertips into the third eye.

30. Bring his or her hand down and angle the fingertips toward the heart while blowing into the heart.

31. Lift the student's fingers to his or her hairline and using the last of the breath, blow over the crown area. Really empty your lungs with this one.

32. Gently place the student's hands in his or her lap.

33. With your hands in heart position, walk to the left around the to student's back. Facing the back of the student, draw the Raku three times. Make this huge, as if you are connecting Spirit, student, and earth.

34. Walk around to the front of your student and draw a huge C, ending by beaming at the heart.

35. Lower your left hand and beam with both hands.

36. Say, "When you are ready, you may open your eyes."

Afterwards, have the student put one hand on top of the other about a foot apart and have him or her turn on the intent to use Reiki. Slowly move your hand between the student's hands so the energy can be felt between the hands. Always check your attunement. This is probably the first time the student has actually felt the energy, and it is a thrilling experience. Remember to remind the student about the changes in his or her energy field and that some detoxification symptoms may be experienced. Tell your students to drink plenty of water to flush the toxins out of the body, pamper themselves, get plenty of rest, and use Reiki on themselves to alleviate the symptoms. The detox process never lasts more than a few days.

First Attunement, Second Degree, Traditional

1. Begin by observing the same opening steps as in the first attunements. After you come back around to the front, hold your fingertips to the student's fingertips and mentally project D, H, S, C one time each.

2. Gently part the student's hands.

3. Place the student's left hand on the lap with the palm up.

4. Cradle the student's right palm flat, face up in your left hand, being careful not to curl your own fingers.

5. With your right hand, draw the C symbol without saying its name over the student's palm.

6. With your right hand open, palm facing down, redraw C, this time saying its name.

7. Gently but firmly slap your right palm onto the student's palm, forcing the C symbol into them.

8. Deeply inhale and exhale, then lower the student's hand back into his or her lap.

9. Pick up the student's left hand, repeat the process.

10. Continue to hold the left hand and pick up the right hand.

11. Place the student's hands together, holding at the wrists.

12. Cup your right hand over the student's fingertips. Silently say D, H, C, S.

13. Hold the student's hands together and gently shake them to give the message that the hands are to stay there.

14. Back away three feet.

15. Place your hands in heart position.

16. With an opened right hand, draw a giant C symbol beginning at eye level, bending your knees to draw the stem to the floor.

17. Complete the C symbol at the student's heart center with opened palm facing the body.

18. Beam at the student's heart chakra for a minute.

19. Step forward and continue beaming.

20. Straddle the student's feet and gently take his or her hands by the wrists as you lift them, angle the fingertips toward the forehead.

21. While inhaling, form the C symbol by drawing it with your tongue.

22. With that same exhale, blow at the third eye, heart, and crown.

23. Close as before.

(Traditional Reiki does not ground the attunements.)

Second Attunement, Second Degree, Traditional

1. Follow the opening attunement, as before.

2. When you come to the front of your student, gently separate his or her hands.

3. Place student's left hand in his or her lap, palm up.

4. Cradle student's right palm flat and facing up with your left hand.

5. With your right hand draw the H symbol, without saying its name.

6. Draw the C symbol while mentally saying the H symbol's name and slap it in.

7. Draw the S symbol without saying its name.

8. Draw the C symbol while saying the S symbol's name and slap it in.

9. Draw the C symbol without saying its name.

10. Draw the C symbol while saying its name and slap it in.

11. Deeply inhale and exhale to make the connection, then lower the student's hand.

12. Pick up the student's left hand and repeat the process.

13. After repeating the process with the left hand, continue to hold the student's left hand and pick up the right hand to join the left.

14. Cup your right hand over the student's fingertips. Silently say the D, H, C, and S symbols.

15. Close as before.

(Traditional Reiki does not ground the attunement.)

Second Degree Attunement, Nontraditional

Explain to the student that he or she will feel you in front and behind. Tell the student that you will be concentrating on and moving his or her hands, and that when you are finished you will ask that he or she open his or her eyes. Emphasize relaxation. Tell the student to close his or her eyes, take a deep breath, and focus on centering.

1. Assume heart position, draw a huge C, and end by beaming at the student's heart. Ask the Reiki guides to attune this student.

2. Walk to the back of the student. Always walk to the right of the student. Place your right hand on his or her right shoulder to equalize the energy. Draw the D, H, C, S symbol one time each.

3. Draw the C symbol over the student's crown with your right hand.

4. Rest your right hand gently on the student's crown, bring your left hand down, and rest it next to the right hand. Draw the D, H, C, S symbols three to four times each.

5. Lift your hands up gently about an inch and check the attunement by feeling the energy flow. The crown should be completely open.

6. Form a triangle with both hands and rest it gently on the occipital region. Draw the D, H, C, S three to four times each.

7. Gently remove your hands; put one hand on each shoulder. Draw the D, H, C, S symbols one time each.

8. Slide your hands down the chest to meet at the heart. Your fingertips should be touching. Draw the D, H, C, S symbols three to four times. Gently lift your hands about an inch off the chest and check the energy flow. The heart should be completely open.

9. With your hands in heart position, walk around to the student's right side.

10. Gently place your right hand over the student's third eye and your left hand over the occipital ridge. Draw the D, H, C, S symbols three to four times each. Gently remove your hands.

11. Walk to the front and straddle the student's feet.

12. Gently separate the student's hands.

13. Place the student's left hand in his or her lap, palm up.

14. Cradle the student's right hand with the palm flat and face up in your left hand.

15. With your right hand draw a C above the student's palm without saying its name.

16. Draw the C symbol with your right palm face down, while mentally saying C, and then slap the symbol into his or her palm. You will end up palm to palm, forcing the symbol into the student's palm.

17. Draw the H symbol above the student's hand, without saying its name.

18. Redraw the H symbol with your palm and repeat the procedure to slap it in.

19. Draw the S symbol above the right hand, without saying its name.

20. Redraw the S symbol with your palm and repeat the procedure to slap it in.

21. Again, draw the C symbol above the right hand without saying its name.

22. Redraw the C symbol with your palm and slap it in.

23. Lower the right hand to the student's lap, palm up, and gently pick up the left hand.

24. Repeat the process (14 through 22) on the left hand.

25. When finished, bring both the student's hands together, palm to palm, and encircle them with your hands. Breathe deeply saying D, H, C, S.

26. Slide the student's fingertips into the first joint of your right hand, and with the left hand in the air draw the D, H, C, and S symbols.

27. Cup the fingertips in your right palm and lift your left hand in the air drawing the D, H, C, S symbols.

28. With your hands on the student's wrists, take a deep breath, and blow gently over and down his or her fingertips.

29. Inhale through your mouth, forming a C with your tongue.

30. Angle the fingertips to the forehead, heart, and crown and blow, as in first attunement.

31. Gently lower the student's hands to the lap.

32. With your hands in heart position, walk to the back and face the student.

33. Draw a huge Raku three times. Remember, you are connecting spirit, student, and earth, so make it vigorous.

34. Walk around to the front, draw a huge C, and end by beaming C into the heart.

35. Lower your left hand down to join your right hand and beam for a minute.

36. Say, "When you are ready, you may open your eyes."

Have the student separate his or her hands and place them on top of each other with palms facing, about a foot apart. Have the student turn on the flow with his or her intent and check the attunement. Again, remember to tell the student about the detoxification process that might be experienced.

Your Masters Attunement

Before I teach you how to pass the master attunement, are you ready for yours? With this attunement you will become a Reiki master. It is a huge privilege for me to pass this attunement on to you. You are becoming a teacher, a master, and a friend, and I honor all three. The bond between us is thick and unbreakable, and I gladly shoulder my responsibility to you. You are loved. Namaste.

I recommend that you read the attunement so you can familiarize yourself with the attunement process. Sit in a comfortable chair, take a deep breath. If you have the video, put the cassette in now.

1. I stand in front of you, channeling the energy and directing it to your entire body.

2. I walk around you and put my right hand on your right shoulder.

3. I work above your crown.

4. I put my hands on the back of your head.

5. I put my hands on both of your shoulders.

6. I put my hands directly over your heart.

7. I walk around to your right side and put one hand on your forehead and one hand on the back of your head.

8. I walk to the front of you and hold your right hand in my left hand.

9. I work over your hand and slap the palm.

10. I press my palm into yours.

11. You feel my breath in your palm.

12. I put your right hand down and pick up your left hand.

13. I work over your hand and slap the palm.

14. I press my palm into yours.

15. You feel my breath in your palm.

16. I put your hands together, palm to palm and envelop your hands with my hands.

17. I breathe down your fingertips into your palms.

18. I raise your hands far over your head, separate the hands, bring them around and back down, putting the hands together again.

19. I point your hands up and hold your fingertips with my hand.

20. I readjust and hold your fingertips with my hand.

21. I angle your fingertips and point to your heart, forehead and crown. You will feel my breath in all three places.

22. I place your hands back in your lap.

23. I walk to the back and ground you.

24. I walk around the front, and you will feel energy in motion.

25. When all is quiet, open your eyes.

Congratulations brand new Reiki master. Go in peace and love.

Namaste, beloved one.

Master Attunement, Non-traditional

I received my master degree in a nontraditional course, so the only attunement I know is the nontraditional one.

1. Assume heart position, facing the student.

2. Draw a large C and end by beaming the heart. Ask Reiki guides to attune this master.

3. Walk around to the back. Always walk to the right of the student.

4. Put your right hand on the studen'ts right shoulder, equalize the energy, and send out D, H, C, S.

5. With your right hand draw all four symbols above the crown.

6. Rest both hands on the crown, and draw the D, H, C, S symbols three to four times each. Check the flow.

7. Form a triangle with your hands and place the triangle on the occipital ridge. Draw the D, H, C, S symbols.

8. Put one hand on each shoulder. Draw the D, H, C, S symbols.

9. Slide your hands down to cover the student's heart, with your fingertips touching. Draw the D, H, C, S symbols three to four times each. Check the flow.

10. Assume heart position and walk to the right until you are at the student's side.

11. Place your right hand on the third eye and your left hand on the occipital ridge. Draw D, H, C, S symbols three to four times each.

12. Assume the heart position and walk to the front of the student. Separate his or her hands.

13. Gently take the student's right hand in your left, with his or her palm facing you.

14. With your right hand draw the D symbol above the hand, without saying its name.

15. Redraw the D symbol with your palm, while saying its name, and slap it into the student's palm, holding your palm there for a minute. Feel the energy flow from you into him or her—master to master.

16. Remove your hand and blow into the student's palm where you have just placed the symbol.

17. Put the right hand down and pick up the left hand.

18. Repeat the process (13 through 16).

19. Place the student's hands together palm to palm and encircle them with your hands. Say D, H, C, S.

20. Point the fingertips upward and blow down and into the closed hands. Send the D, H, C, S symbols.

21. With hands still together, take the student's wrists and raise the hands out and up above his or her head. Separate the hands and bring them down and around to rejoin palm to palm in front. This is done joyfully.

22. Point the hands up and grab the student's fingertips with the first digit of your right hand. Raise your left hand up in air. Send the D, H, C, and S symbols.

23. Readjust the student's hands and swing the fingertips into the palm of your right hand. Your left hand is in the air. Send the D, H, C, and S symbols.

24. Take a deep breath, form a C in your mouth, and angle the student's fingertips toward their heart, forehead, and crown. Blow breath in each place. Expel all your excess breath on the student's crown.

25. Place the student's hands gently back in his or her lap.

26. Walk around the back and draw huge Raku. Remember, you are joining Source, human, and earth. Perform this three times with zest.

27. Walk to the front of the student and draw a huge C with right hand, ending by beaming toward the heart.

28. Lower your left hand and continue beaming at heart.

29. Say, "When you are ready, you may open your eyes."

Always check the attunement by having the student separate his or her hands, palm facing palm, and turn on the intent. Feel the flow of energy.

SUMMARY

In this section you have learned the meaning of the word master and that you must live your life so all who come in contact with you will know that you are a Reiki master.

You have studied the seven spiritual bodies and have learned to work with and within these bodies to prevent dis-ease from manifesting in the physical body.

You have learned how to compose your course material. It is important that you practice Reiki as a master before you begin to teach. This course is only the tip of the iceberg of the lessons that await you in your Reiki practice.

You have some suggestions of where you may find locations to teach your classes and how to advertise your classes. The value of a fair exchange for services has been reiterated here.

You have been taught the attunement process and how to pass attunements. With practice, this will become very easy. Remember, there is no wrong way to pass an attunement. If it is your intention to attune the student, the attunement is valid.

You have received your Master attunement, which radically changed your energy field. Your hands are now the hands of one who can attune others to continue the tradition of Reiki.

I am very proud of you.

Namaste Beloved One

> There is a destiny
> that makes us brothers
> None goes his way alone.
> All that we send into
> the lives of others
> Comes back into our own.
>
> —Markham, Leaves of Gold

All things must come to an end, and it is with sorrow that I complete this book. Although you and I have never met face to face, I feel I know you through the attunement process. Receiving your attunements via text and or video does not negate the spiritual bond that is formed between master and student during the attunement process. My soul recognizes and loves your soul. It is a great honor and privilege for me to have had the opportunity to guide you in your Reiki path. I honor you.

Now it is time for you to go and teach and learn and teach and learn, and so it is. You have the knowledge and ability and are a very powerful master. Use this ability wisely. As always, I am here for you.

There is such a need for healing on this planet of ours. I feel very strongly that the only way we are going to have peace on earth and goodwill toward each other is for each of us to heal ourselves, heal others, and then teach others to heal themselves. To think of healing the whole planet often staggers the imagination, but if we think of healing one person at a time it becomes a possibility. This planet can only be healed one person at a time, and I trust each of you, as Reiki masters, to go out and continue the process I have started with this book.

Let us join hands across the world, and in so doing heal ourselves and our brothers and sisters, in each and every country.

The God in me recognizes and honors the God in you and is full of joy to have shared this time with you.

> I now turn away from the world about me and enter the world of my consciousness. I allow no memories of the past to dwell here, and I create no images of the future. This is my time and place to concentrate on my being. I allow myself to gently slide into the deepest recesses of my being. My soul is at peace, in perfect repose. I know this is my immortal self, and I see myself as I am—eternal, immortal, perfect. I always was and I always will be. All others are but a mirror image of myself. I am bound to each soul, and each soul is bound to me. Together we create our universe. All meet and unite within me. I am pure spirit, I am birthless, deathless, and changeless. I am for all time and contain the knowledge of all things. I have no beginning and no end, I am the font of all abundance, and I am the creator of all life. Whenever I desire, I become one with the Source of all creation. For it is this very Source who has created me, who dwells within me, who orchestrates my very existence. I am Source and Source is me. I am.

> Namaste beloved one.
> Barbara

About the Author

Barbara Emerson has been a Reiki master since 1995. She has dedicated the past several years of her life to finding a means of providing Reiki attunements to people who don't have access or enough money to attend a course.

Emerson made a life-changing commitment to Reiki when she experienced the healing techniques of Reiki personally. She has devised her own system of passing attunements because of her conviction that everyone should benefit from the healing power of Reiki. Emerson lives in Arizona, where she maintains a Reiki practice.